BRIAN ENO'S
Ambient 1: Music for Airports

Oxford KEYNOTES

Series Editor KEVIN C. KARNES

Sergei Prokofiev's Alexander Nevsky
KEVIN BARTIG

Claude Debussy's Clair de Lune
GURMINDER KAUR BHOGAL

Rodgers and Hammerstein's Carousel
TIM CARTER

Aaron Copland's Appalachian Spring
ANNEGRET FAUSER

Arlen and Harburg's Over the Rainbow
WALTER FRISCH

Arvo Pärt's Tabula Rasa
KEVIN C. KARNES

Beethoven's Symphony No. 9
ALEXANDER REHDING

Brian Eno's Ambient 1: Music for Airports
JOHN T. LYSAKER

BRIAN ENO'S *Ambient 1: Music for Airports*

JOHN T. LYSAKER

OXFORD UNIVERSITY PRESS

Oxford University Press is a department of the University of Oxford. It furthers the University's objective of excellence in research, scholarship, and education by publishing worldwide. Oxford is a registered trade mark of Oxford University Press in the UK and certain other countries.

Published in the United States of America by Oxford University Press
198 Madison Avenue, New York, NY 10016, United States of America.

Library of Congress Cataloging-in-Publication Data
Names: Lysaker, John T. author.
Title: Brian Eno's Ambient 1: Music for airports / John T. Lysaker.
Description: New York, NY : Oxford University Press, 2019. |
Series: Oxford keynotes | Includes bibliographical references and index.
Identifiers: LCCN 2018012165 | ISBN 9780190497293 (hardcover : alk. paper) |
ISBN 9780190497309 (pbk. : alk. paper)
Subjects: LCSH: Eno, Brian, 1948– Music for airports.
Classification: LCC ML410.E58 L97 2019 | DDC 786.7—dc23
LC record available at https://lccn.loc.gov/2018012165

For Steven Brence and Jeff Stolle

Series Editor's INTRODUCTION

Oxford Keynotes reimagines the canons of Western music for the twenty-first century. With each of its volumes dedicated to a single composition or album, the series provides an informed, critical, and provocative companion to music as artwork and experience. Books in the series explore how works of music have engaged listeners, performers, artists, and others through history and in the present. They illuminate the roles of musicians and musics in shaping Western cultures and societies, and they seek to spark discussion of ongoing transitions in contemporary musical landscapes. Each approaches its key work in a unique way, tailored to the distinct opportunities that the work presents. Targeted at performers, curious listeners, and advanced undergraduates, volumes in the series are written by expert and engaging voices in their fields, and will therefore be of significant interest to scholars and critics as well.

In selecting titles for the series, Oxford Keynotes balances two ways of defining the canons of Western music: as lists of works that critics and scholars deem to have articulated key moments in the history of the art, and as lists of works that comprise the bulk of what consumers listen to, purchase, and perform today. Often, the two lists intersect, but the overlap is imperfect. While not neglecting the first, Oxford Keynotes gives considerable weight to the second. It confronts the musicological canon with the living repertoire of performance and recording in classical, popular, jazz, and other idioms. And it seeks to expand that living repertoire through the latest musicological research.

Kevin C. Karnes
Emory University

CONTENTS

ABOUT THE COMPANION WEBSITE

Oxford University Press has created a website to accompany *Brian Eno's Ambient 1: Music for Airports* that features audio clips of many musical passages discussed over the course of the book. It also includes one video clip that provides a glimpse of one of Eno's video paintings. Readers are encouraged to consult this resource while working through the chapters. This will enrich their experience of the book and *Ambient 1: Music for Airports.* Files available online are indicated in the text with Oxford's symbol ▶.

www.oup.com/us/bea1
Username: Music1
Password: Book5983

The reader is invited to explore the full catalogue of Oxford Keynotes volumes on the series homepage.
www.oup.com/us/oxfordkeynotes

ACKNOWLEDGMENTS

This short text has had a lot of friends. The Office of the Dean in Emory University's College of Arts and Sciences enabled me to hire a research assistant, Lilly Levy, who was invaluable in tracking down interviews, images, and secondary literature. Joe Benavides also helped me organize the notes and bibliography, Ben Davis helped with the index, and Michael Kim helped me locate some images when deadlines were imminent. Thanks to all.

The Fox Center for Humanistic Inquiry provided me with time and an office during the academic year of 2015–16. It was during this period that my research for the book began in earnest. A big thank you to Tina, Steve, Amy, and Colette. Thanks also to the participants in my four-part, eight-hour seminar on *Music for Airports*, which took place at the Center during November 2016.

I test-drove some early thoughts at a meeting of the American Philosophies Forum. This was a great prod in the right direction, and comments from other participants proved useful as the project developed, as did the opportunity to concretize those remarks in an article, "Turning

Listening Inside Out," which appeared in the *Journal of Speculative Philosophy.*

Near the close of the project I emailed some questions to Evan Ziporyn, a founding member of the Bang on a Can All-Stars. He was generous with his time and thoughtful. The tasks (and concerns) of the critic-theorist and the artist are quite different, and the two often meet in strained circumstances. (A critic is to art as a pigeon is to statues, I've been told.) Evan, however, seemed genuinely jazzed to think about *Music for Airports*, and that was useful and just plain fun.

Various people and offices at the Woodruff Library, Emory University, were very helpful along the way. I was at a loss with regard to finding old articles from rock magazines, and James Steffen, the film studies and media librarian, generously helped me locate key articles that I then accessed through the excellent Interlibrary Loan office. The Emory Center for Digital Scholarship also helped me scan images and prepare files for the companion website. I am grateful to the several student workers who aided me along the way.

A PhD in philosophy is poor training for tracking down images and securing permission to employ them. Everyone I contacted was unfailingly helpful and generous. As you come across the images that follow, please hear a "thank you" to those depicted and/or their representatives.

Several discussions of genuine merit and insight await anyone who elects to write on Eno. Those I've encountered share recordings, remarks by Eno, and questions of mutual concern. Because my audience is principally general and not academic, my engagement with that scholarship is limited, particularly where disagreements could arise. But I have benefited from the scholarship, which I've noted throughout. However, I want to acknowledge my gratitude beyond those notes, particularly for the writings of Geeta Dayal, David Sheppard, Cecilia Sun, Eric Tamm, and David Toop, none of whom I know but all of whom have proven good company. (You'll find the titles of their books alongside others in the section called Additional Sources for Reading and Listening.) I must also thank the tireless laborers that maintain two websites: MORE DARK THAN SHARK and EnoWeb. Each has gathered numerous interviews that are resources for scholars and fans alike.

Other support was literally more material. Several record and CD shops have kept me flush since I first fell for music around 1980. I name them with gratitude and pleasure: the Princeton Record Exchange; the House of Records in Eugene, Oregon; and now several in the greater Atlanta area—Criminal Records, Decatur CD, Ella Guru, and Mojo Vinyl. A good shop curates as well as stocks, and I've been the beneficiary of many top-flight curators. (Our neighborhood postman, David Bomar, also brought many LPs and CDs, and always asked how the book was coming along, which was much appreciated.)

I'm one whose love of music generated a love for the kind of equipment that can make it sing. Echo Audio in Portland, Oregon, has been my dealer for what is almost twenty years, and I thank them—particularly Kurt Doslu—every time the needle drops or I press play. In particular, Kurt's old turntable brought *Music for Airports* to life in new and startling ways.

My beloved wife, Hilary Hart, was, as in everything, a boon companion throughout the writing process, which occasionally left me distracted, puzzled and puzzling, and probably for the birds (as opposed to airports). Our marriage is an ongoing joy, and her indulgence was very much appreciated.

Kevin Karnes has proven a great interlocutor along the way, whether in response to writing or in conversation. I probably never would have pursued the project without his prodding, and it would have been worse off without his feedback and willingness to hear me riff on some recent discovery or, as was more often the case, confusion.

Finally, my ear for music changed radically when I began to make my own with Steven Brence, Jeff Stolle, and John Capaccio, and then later with Steve, Jeff, John Fenn, and Ben Saunders. I began to hear so much more, and to hear choices made (and resisted) in the music of others. And I got a feel for how sounds present a kind of meaning that resists translation into discursive prose, which I hope informs what follows. Furthermore, trying, alongside Jeff Stolle, to write songs that didn't embarrass us (or those who heard them) made me a good deal humbler in the face of whatever music catches my ear. I can't thank the lads enough, Jeff and Steven most of all. They let an untutored ear and throat into their midst and that reopened a world I thought I knew.

BRIAN ENO'S
Ambient 1: Music for Airports

INTRODUCTION

WHITE NOISE, SEMINAL SOUNDS

I've decided to turn the word "pretentious" into a compliment.
—Eno, *A Year With Swollen Appendices*

In 1978, Brian Eno released *Ambient 1: Music for Airports* on LP and cassette.[1] Four tracks grace its two sides: "1/1," "2/1," "1/2," and "2/2." Lyrics are not involved. Instead, each track organizes clusters of sounds that repeat at irregular intervals and without any backing rhythms. Not only is it impossible to sing along, none of the tracks sustain the attention they initially gather. And yet it remains too interesting to ignore.

An insert provides a miniature manifesto. It explicates "ambient." Likening the LP to Muzak, Eno offers *Music for Airports* (*MFA*) as an "atmosphere, or a surrounding influence: a tint." The music should "accommodate many levels of attention without enforcing one in particular."[2] This recalls Darius Milhaud's characterization of Erik Satie's *musique d'ameublement*, or "musical furniture—music to be

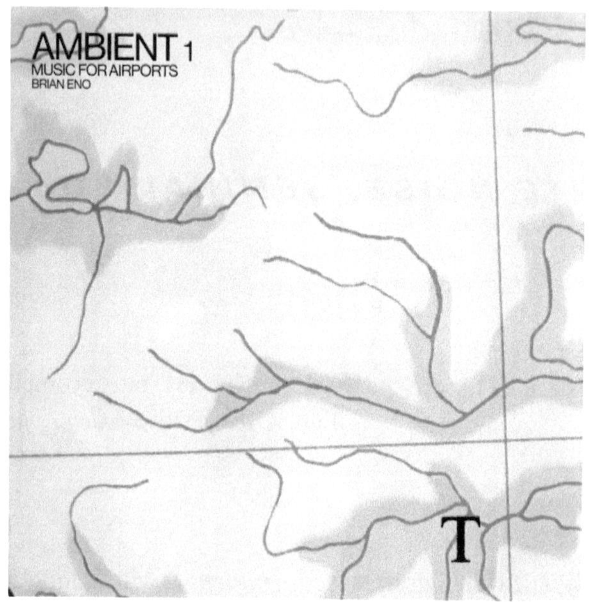

FIGURE 0.1 The front cover of *MFA*

heard but not listened to."[3] Eno seems to be saying: it could be that, but it could also be something more. But what? Unlike Muzak, which was designed to improve productivity, Eno's ambient venture "is intended to induce calm and a space to think," as the liner notes further state—an intriguing suggestion, one you might explore and test by playing the album as you read.

When *MFA* appeared, Eno's name was everywhere. A darling of the musical press since his time in Roxy Music, he had since leaving the band released four solo albums, including *Another Green World* (1975), which led Charley Walters of *Rolling Stone* to announce: "Eno insists on risks, and that they so consistently pan out is a major triumph.

FIGURE 0.2 The label of a Japanese pressing of *MFA,* side one

I usually shudder at such a description, but *Another Green World* is indeed an important record—and also a brilliant one."[4] Eno had also produced albums by Devo and Talking Heads and collaborated on David Bowie's *Low* and *Heroes*, albums whose influence quickly spread across a pop scene split, even fragmented, by the full arrival of punk in 1976. But *MFA* was rarely reviewed. *Rolling Stone* gave it passing notice without praise. "As aesthetic white noise, *Ambient 1: Music for Airports* makes for even more dissipated listening than last year's similarly unfocused *Music for Films*."[5] As Eno himself noted in 1996: "Like a lot of the stuff I was doing at the time, this was regarded by many English music critics as a kind of arty joke, and they had a lot of fun with

AMBIENT 1
MUSIC FOR AIRPORTS
BRIAN ENO
ミュージック・フォー・エアーポート
イーノ

AMBIENT MUSIC

The concept of music designed specifically as a background feature in the environment was pioneered by Muzak Inc. in the fifties, and has since come to be known generically by the term Muzak. The connotations that this term carries are those particularly associated with the kind of material that Muzak Inc. produces – familiar tunes arranged and orchestrated in a lightweight and derivative manner. Understandably, this has led most discerning listeners (and most composers) to dismiss entirely the concept of environmental music as an idea worthy of attention.

Over the past three years, I have become interested in the use of music as ambience, and have come to believe that it is possible to produce material that can be used thus without being in any way compromised. To create a distinction between my own experiments in this area and the products of the various purveyors of canned music, I have begun using the term Ambient Music.

An ambience is defined as an atmosphere, or a surrounding influence: a tint. My intention is to produce original pieces ostensibly (but not exclusively) for particular times and situations with a view to building up a small but versatile catalogue of environmental music suited to a wide variety of moods and atmospheres.

Whereas the extant canned music companies proceed from the basis of regularizing environments by blanketing their acoustic and atmospheric idiosyncracies, Ambient Music is intended to enhance these. Whereas conventional background music is produced by stripping away all sense of doubt and uncertainty (and thus all genuine interest) from the music, Ambient Music retains these qualities. And whereas their intention is to 'brighten' the environment by adding stimulus to it (thus supposedly alleviating the tedium of routine tasks and levelling out the natural ups and downs of the body rhythms) Ambient Music is intended to induce calm and a space to think.

Ambient Music must be able to accommodate many levels of listening attention without enforcing one in particular; it must be as ignorable as it is interesting.

BRIAN ENO
September 1978

FIGURE 0.3 Liner notes to *MFA*

it."[6] And not just critics; some of Eno's peers disliked the album. Lydia Lunch, a fixture in New York's "no wave" music scene, which Eno had helped promote, reportedly snarked: "it is just something that flows and weaves, flows and weaves . . . it's kind of nauseating. It's like drinking a glass of water. It means nothing, but it's very smooth going down."[7]

Times change. *MFA* is now a touchstone work within and beyond a genre it helped found. Michael Bloom, writing for *Pitchfork* in 2004, reviewed several Eno albums

FIGURE 0.4 Brian Eno, as painted by Tom Phillips. Copyright Tom Phillips/Dacs.

and awarded *MFA* a 9.2/10. In 2016, Ivan Hewitt, the classical music critic for the *Telegraph*, credited Eno with the invention of ambient music, terming it a "seismic moment in musical history."[8] In my view, artists don't invent genres but guide currents into more forceful streams, which others then discover and ride, as many have done with the category "ambient." But something remarkable did occur with *MFA*, which was the first musical work entitled "ambient" in a generic manner. In fact, its proper title is *Ambient 1*, the first in a series of four. And the term caught on, even morphed. There are now multiple subgenres of ambient music, moving from minimal, reverberating drones, so-called "isolationism," into danceable numbers that helped constitute IDM—intelligent dance music—and on toward the offshoot, "illbient," which layers hip-hop beats, samples, and the kind of long, drawn-out tones often associated with ambient music. But *MFA* remains something of a reference point. In 2008, Tony Marcus, writing for *FACT*, listed *MFA* first in a series of the twenty "greatest ambient records of all time," and in 2016 *MFA* ranked first in Pitchfork's "50 Best Ambient Albums of All Time." Not that all accept the album hook, line, and sinker. The Black Dog, a group from Sheffield, England, thought a musical rebuttal was in order. *Music for Real Airports* (2010) aims to contrast the perceived serenity of Eno's album with moods and sonic shapes more in line with how "airports tend to reduce us to worthless pink blobs of flesh."[9]

MFA also resonates outside pop circles, and with the kind of contestation that accompanies seminal works. The experimental music ensemble Bang on a Can scored it for acoustic instruments in 1999 and proceeded to perform and record their interpretations. (More recently, other ensembles have done the same with Eno's *Discreet Music* and *Apollo*, and Bang on a Can continues to perform *MFA*, as at their fifteenth annual festival in July 2016.) And in something of a counter thrust, Psychic Temple, a jazz ensemble rotating around the direction of Chris Schlarb, has recorded an improvisational reading of the album's first track. "1/1," Schlarb explains, is "like patient jazz improvisation, with a surprising, organic quality that reminds me of the Bill Evans Trio with Paul Motian and Scott LeFaro. Unfortunately,

FIGURE 0.5 The front cover of *Music for Real Airports*. Design By Human.

like jazz, it has become a museum piece, something to be analyzed by select musicians inside expensive concert halls. I wanted to rescue it from that dark, boring fate."[10]

This short study is for listeners who want to think and reflect upon what Eno's LP has to offer, and in a way that deepens future listening rather than replaces it with scholarly prose. The goal is not to offer a definitive analysis of the work's compositional structure nor an exhaustive or even thorough account of the historical conditions surrounding its creation and reception. Nor is my focus Eno's unorthodox but palpable genius. Instead, I wonder: What confronts us when we play the album? To what should we listen? And

FIGURE 0.6 Bang on a Can All Stars performing *MFA* in the Dusseldorf airport. Photo by Kenny Savelson/Bang on a Can.

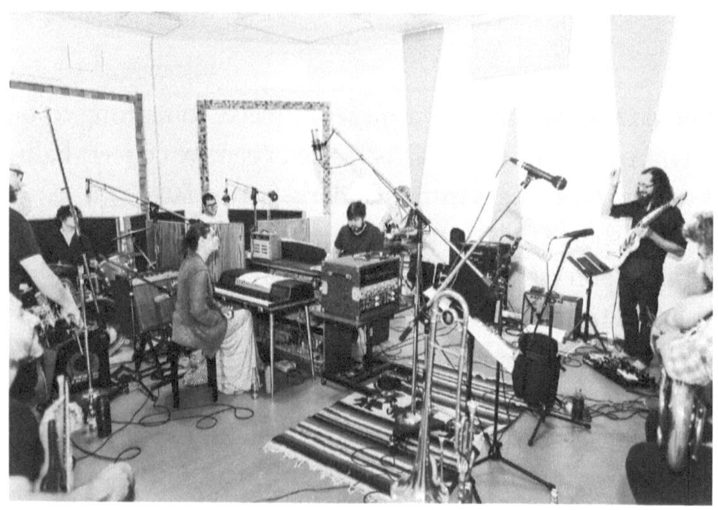

FIGURE 0.7 Psychic Temple session shot

what should we have in mind as we do? A passing knowledge of Eno leads one into names like John Cage, La Monte Young, and Steve Reich. How should we think about the influence of avant-garde art music in relation to an LP by a former member of the glam rock troupe Roxy Music? What and who else is pertinent?

Five chapters and an afterward follow. They blend musical and historical analysis with occasional philosophical reflections on what "music" means in a context as provocative as the one convened by *MFA*. The lists are far from comprehensive, but they should give readers a feel for MFA's various musical contexts. (Parts of that music, marked in the text by ▶, are available for listeners on the companion website for this book.) A fuller discography is provided at the close of the book in the section entitled "Additional Sources for Reading and Listening."

Chapter 1 explores the general sonic character of *MFA*. What does one find when one simply listens and listens simply? Because the tracks are devoid of standard musical patterns (melody, harmony, and rhythm, for example), chapter 2 situates the album in what might be termed the "sonic turn," a move away from traditional Western musical structures toward sounds, whether found and/or manipulated.

While Eno seemed to enter music through rock 'n' roll, Eno's ambient venture is very much a piece of twentieth-century avant-garde musical practice. Chapter 3 thus explores how Eno came to set up shop at this crossroad, how he became a self-styled "non-musician." Chapter 4 then takes up the idea of "ambient music," situating *MFA* along a historical continuum and focusing on what happens to music when it functions ambiently, and what happens to us in the ambient clutch of *MFA*.

Eno's album also functions as conceptual art—art that reflects and comments on its own standing and purpose as "art." Chapter 5 explores *MFA*'s conceptual dimensions, from its status as "generative music" to its exemplification of a certain conception of art and art's relation to life and nature. Because *MFA*'s conceptual enactment directs listeners toward their own reception, chapter 5 also reflects on the kinds of listening the album invites, including when it is scored for and performed on instruments.

If you noticed that a handful of my concerns are principally philosophical, you may have also wondered: Won't philosophy prove rude and clumsy in the context of a work that shimmers and resounds as elusively as *MFA*? I would caution against distinguishing, too readily and too thoroughly, the sensible from the intelligible, the sensuous from concepts that threaten to subdue it. Such distinctions prove unstable simply by being named. More importantly, such distinctions, at least when strictly opposed, fall short of what *MFA* achieves. Eno came to his ambient work through a heady art-school scene as averse to things without ideas as W. C. Williams was averse to the reverse—"No ideas but in things," he proclaimed in *Patterson* (1927). Second, in conversation with John Brockman, Eno has confessed to a double life: "Part of my life of course is being an artist, but the other part, just as interesting to me, is wondering what it is I'm doing."[11] These two "parts" interact in *MFA*. Some music makes you dance. *Ambient 1* makes you think, and in more ways than one, which prompts more thinking.

CHAPTER 1

A FIRST LISTEN, OR THROUGH A GLASS LIGHTLY

There are far more types of sounds that aren't musical in a traditional sense. They're not sounds that you connect with any particular instrument or with any particular object.

— Eno, in *Downbeat: The Great Jazz Interviews*

Music for Airports is an album of tracks: "1/1" and "2/1," "1/2," and "2/2." Their titles do not provide much in the way of direction. In fact, they only tell us what we already know if we have the LP in our hands—there are two tracks per side. The title of the album is no less perplexing. In what way is this *for* airports? Are we to think of airports, of being there, of traveling? Richard Strauss's *Alpine Symphony* scores a journey into the mountains. The opening sections bear the subtitles "Night," "Sunrise," and "The Ascent," which the music conveys. The ascent offers notes ascending, and the murky swirl of "Night" gives way to the increased dynamics and brassy rays of "Sunrise." What of Eno's record?

Consider the back side of the album cover. In the manner of twentieth-century avant-garde "scores," such as Earle Brown's *4 Systems*, each track is given a box, and various marks are used in place of notes. I take this to suggest that whatever sounds accord with these marks, they do not primarily belong to the twelve notes of the Western chromatic scale. Brown specifies a keyboard—indicated by four sets of parallel, continuous lines—but one is invited to follow the notation in "any sequence, either side up," with thickness indicating dynamics or clusters. One can thus play the piano while ignoring keys, common chords, and typical harmonic relations, say by striking a fistful of black and white keys somewhere near the middle-left of the keyboard. One needn't, but one could, and that indicates that one is playing with a set of sounds much larger than the range of pitches available to composers writing for typical Western instruments tuned in traditional ways. Moreover, one is free to combine them in ways that fall outside equally typical keys and harmonic orders. And should one make sounds within those orders—one seems welcome to do so—the result will still resonate, at least in part, beyond those orders. Brown's score sets itself within the possibilities open to the piano at hand. Put differently, whatever one plays will be sounds of a piano, much like a coconut has a sound, or one's desk, rather than a note in a given key.

Because they do not refer to any instruments, Eno's marks are even more obscure than Brown's. Moreover, they are not instructions for performers, given that the album was assembled from tape loops and synthesizer overdubs.

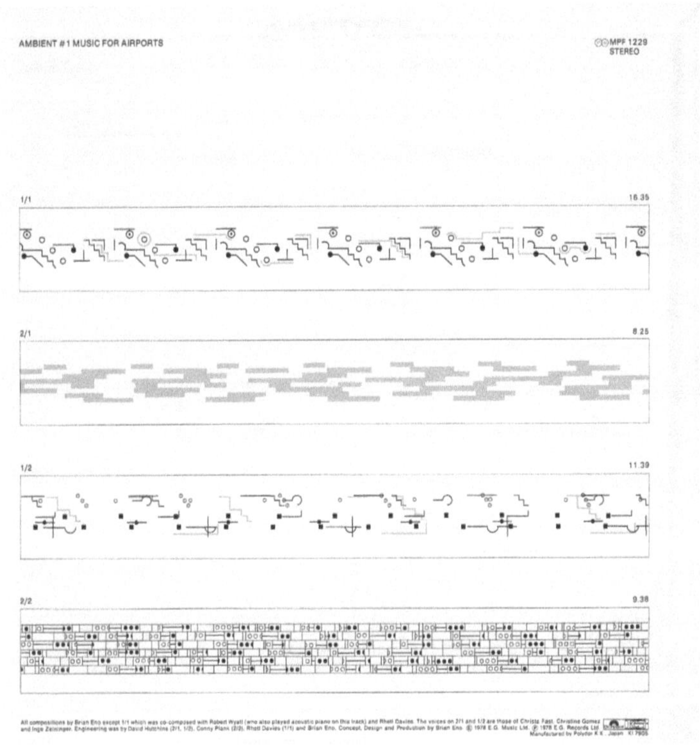

FIGURE 1.1 The back cover of *MFA*

A tape loop involves the continual repetition of musical material on a run of magnetic tape that has been cut and reattached or spliced together, thus forming a loop that plays on a reel-to-reel machine until stopped. In the case of "1/1," which contains sounds from two pianos, the parts were initially recorded as improvisational exercises.[1] Eno liked a short bit where the two piano parts interacted when mixed together. (The players were improvising independently of one another, as were two other musicians on bass and guitar.) Eno cut the segment of tape that captivated

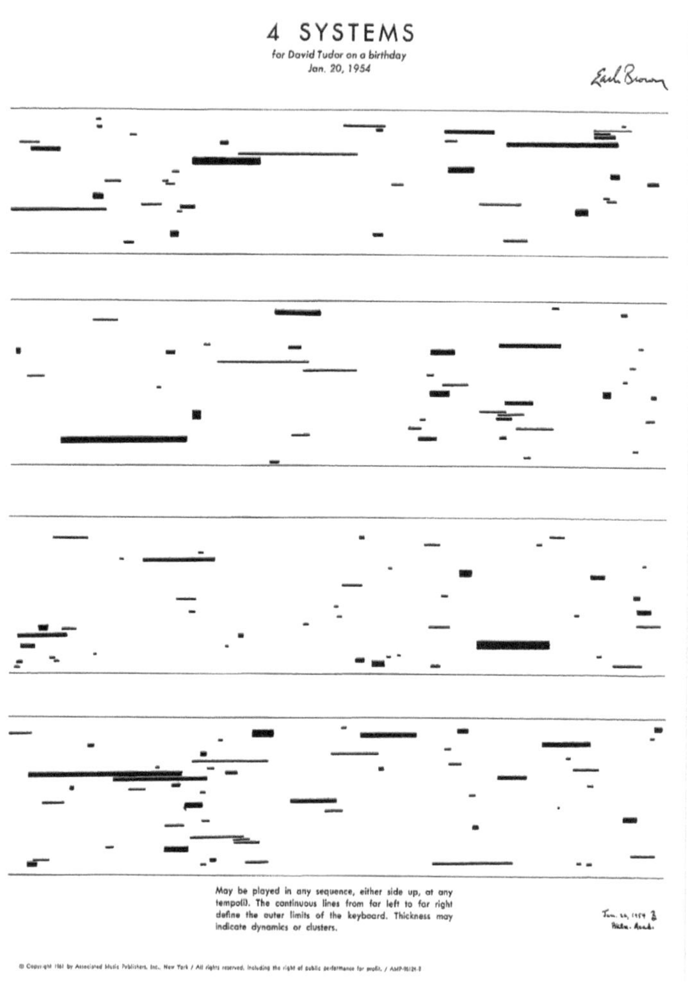

FIGURE 1.2 An excerpt from Earle Brown, *Folio and 4 Systems* (1954). Courtesy of the Earle Brown Music Foundation, Rye, NY.

him, ignored the bass and guitar tracks he also had, and created a loop that he elected to play at half speed, preferring a rounder tone from the pianos and overall slower pace. "1/1," therefore, does not represent the performance of

FIGURE 1.3 Earle Brown with the score of *Indices*. Courtesy of the Earle Brown Music Foundation, Rye, NY.

a scored piece or even a part of a piece. Nor does it capture the improvisational interplay of two musicians. Instead, it is music composed from tape for tape.

The tracks on *MFA* involve more than single tape loops, however. Various loops were created and allowed to play together in various ways, but without any underlying rhythmic structure to govern their interactions. As Eno says of "2/1," the loops would "repeat in cycles that are incommensurable—they are not likely to come back into sync again."[2] *MFA* thus presents us with sounds freed from any score and assembled without an underlying rhythm. In large measure, it is an assemblage of tape loops interacting rather than the aural record of musicians performing a score. And that presents listeners with sounds that belong together in ways that elude without rigorously avoiding the customary feel for phenomena like pitch, chords, keys, harmony, and rhythm that orient so much of the Western musical tradition.

MFA is thus a strange work of music. And it is that strangeness that Eno's diagrams seem to underscore. Directed at the listener, they announce: fresh ears are needed for what awaits. Yes, these are sounds ordered in time. (Each block is tagged with an overall time.) And their relations will have a character worth tracking, each graphically marked on the "score." For example, "2/1" promises shifts in slightly varied blocks of sound, whereas "2/2" promises a very dense network of sounds. But that doesn't really instruct our attention in the manner of a score, which tells us what we should play (or hear). Instead, Eno's scores direct our attention without really focusing it, which suggests that they are more an invitation than a set of instructions.

The aesthetic feel of "1/1" is gentle, patient, and somewhat charming, meaning that bits are beguiling—they catch the ear, like the descending piano phrase around 1′12″ that recalls the lullaby "Frère Jacques" (▶ Audio 1.1). Across the whole, there is a discernible piano part of sorts. One first hears it over the opening twelve seconds or so—six notes roll down and then rise, followed by a three-note line on a second piano, which is succeeded by a four-note descending echo on the first piano, which repeats four notes from the middle of the opening phrase. (Example 1.1)

The second piano, an electric one, chimes in every now and then, sometimes with a quick phrase or a chord, like one at 0′12″, which continues to ring for over ten seconds.

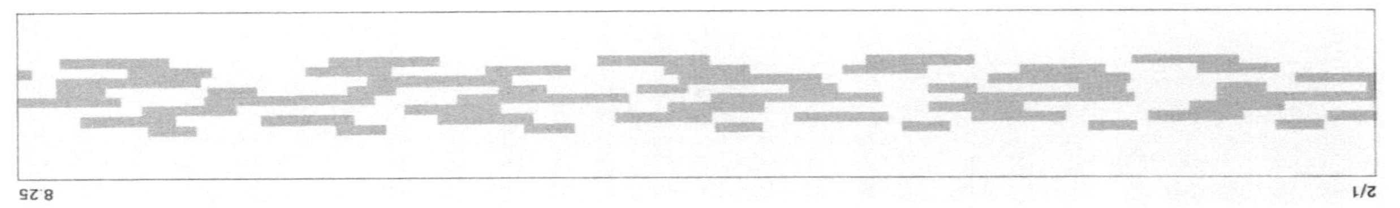

FIGURE 1.4 The "score" for "2/1."

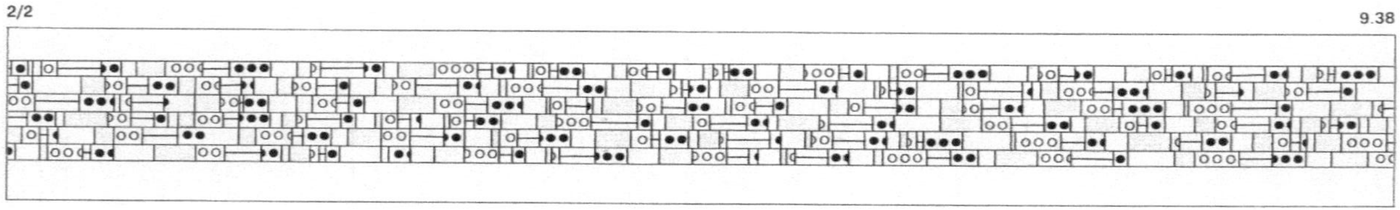

FIGURE 1.5 The "score" for "2/2."

EXAMPLE 1.1 Recurring part for two pianos, 1/1

Neither piano part develops, however. In fact, except for the echo of "Frère Jacques," nothing effectively sustains a melody. And that sense of something just short of a melody is intensified by breaks of several seconds marked only by a lingering sustain that, as it persists, draws attention away from its predecessors and focuses us upon its own decay, texture, and dynamic.[3] Not that a kind of monotony takes over; as tones and tonal relations give way to others, there is little if any repetition. Across the first minute, the piano phrase in example 1.1 recurs three times, but never in the same way and for the same length of time. Listening, one hears notes rise and fall continuously, and while nothing jars by way of dynamic surges or pronounced tonal shifts; each arrival has a novel feel.

Thinking more of the whole, one notices how the notes hang in a musical space not unlike that of a painting, as many have noted—a shape here, a color there, each juxtaposed, but without an audible logic to link them.[4] But the analogy to painting, which Eno himself employs, can mislead if a neatly delineated, perspectival space is presumed. The sustained tones sometimes swell and recede, blurring differences between background and foreground. (▶ Audio 1.2) This is space (or place) on the move, and it unfolds over the course of the audible duration of the piece, which lasts for about sixteen and a half minutes, though the back cover indicates a duration of 16′39″, suggesting that something continues, just out of our reach. The result is thus more like a natural space than a painting—phenomena pass by at different speeds and continue after our attention has shifted elsewhere. And note, the sounds and moods of an airport are not in play in any clear manner. Rather, the sounds are insistently that—sounds, together and alone. And then there is silence. Not a rest, but a long silence that, in the case of the end of "1/1," gives the digital track a total time of 17′22″.

Sonically, "2/1" is almost all breath. The voices of Christa Fast, Christine Gomez, and Inge Zeininger as well as Eno are layered atop one another as they sing "ahhhhh." The first grouping unfolds over forty seconds or so, the second closing at 1′35″ or so, and there are other points where the voices give way to silence. Single, sustaining tones from a synthesizer occasionally appear behind the voices, complementing and thereby thickening the tones without offering an obvious harmonic foundation for the whole. And again, there is a kind of space in which each "ahhhhh" maintains a character of its own, even when they blend. "2/1" is thus painterly in the way "1/1" is, presenting juxtapositions (and blends) rather than melodic developments. In this regard, the score that Eno offers on the back cover is quite apt: blocks of sound, presented as such, sometimes atop one another. The silences are more apparent than they were in "1/1," however, as between 3′12″ and 3′16″. And their arrival does not bring rhythmic energy to the track in the manner of a rest or beats in a measure. In fact, the procession does not seem bound to any rhythm. Yes, the track unfolds temporally, but not in a manner that one can predict, which halts one's anticipations to a point of greater receptiveness (or distraction). "2/1" also avoids appreciable dynamics. The music isn't quiet so much as relaxed, and it never startles with abrupt rises or drops in volume. The voices are thus birdlike in their passing. They float—a quality achieved, in part, by their reverbed breathiness, which sounds unearthly without being heavenly, particularly on digital files, which have a slight edge to the attack of the vocal tones.

The floating voices of "1/2" are the nearest thing to programmatic elements in *MFA*—something like the shared wonder of people flying. But the voices could be wondering about anything. And that is true of the album as a whole. Nothing seems particularly tied to airports, or anything for that matter, which distinguishes it from *Music for Airport Furniture* (2011) by Stephen Whittington (b. 1953), scored for string quartet. In a statement that seems to have anchored a press release, he says: "I was interested in the airport departure lounge as an arena for human emotions—boredom, apprehension, hope, despair, loneliness, the tenderness of farewell—all taking place within a bland, often desolate space."[5] And one doesn't have to work hard to hear those moods, some of which are set off by full rests, as at 12′48″ and 15′38″. The opening minute or so is plaintive, and functions like a long shot in a film, setting a scene that is fairly bleak. It is then followed by minutes of what could be boredom, indicated by slow violin tones drawn without appreciable dynamics. And other moods follow. A deep longing is apparent after 13′30″,

FIGURE 1.6 Stephen Whittington

and it gives way to despair by 14′58″ (▶ Audio 1.3). In contrast, *MFA* conveys little if any emotion. The "ahhhhs" of "1/2" never swell, surge, or empty out. Instead, they mark a slight, modest attention, but without providing any clues regarding their object. If they call attention to anything, therefore, it is more to their own occurrence than to whatever drew their fancy.

The elements one finds in "1/1" and "2/1" combine in "1/2." Voices resonate in simple tones with a similar ethereal quality, though they occur less frequently. In the first five of what will be a twelve-minute track, they occur in three groupings: 0′15″–0′50″, 1′14″–1′48″, and commencing again at 4′54″. They are again layered, subjected to reverb, and clustered, which is to say they overlap, but in a manner unsubordinated to established harmonies. They also are offset by a more consistent interplay between a piano whose notes preserve, lightly, the link between the key and the hammer and an electric piano occupying a lower tonal register and playing a sparser part. The track begins with a quick succession of notes on the piano, followed by three seconds of silence, followed by a searching, improvisational piano sequence, complemented by the entry of the electric piano with a descending line that begins at the five-second point, ends at eleven seconds, and rings until after the voices enter, eventually fading into them at about twenty seconds. And "fading in" is an apt description of how they relate. The voices and pianos (and occasional synth tone) interact in ways that give "1/2" a meditative mood, which hovers in the absence of a clear rhythm.

Other tracks also conjure moods, but "1/2" sounds more integrated, though the tones neither work together like instruments in a chamber setting, developing lines of musical thought, nor establish a tonal background, whether for variations on a theme or refined explorations of a key. Instead, they sound like distinct sonic lines that occasionally overlap. Moreover, they are intensively simple—zero virtuosity is on display. One could imagine almost anyone playing the piano parts after being told to improvise on the keyboard, keep it simple and gentle, and work with very small units of sound. So too the sung parts, particularly given how the reverb smooths the pitch. The distinctness of any voice and its relative accuracy is erased in the treatments. As a whole, then, the tones of "1/2" are modestly organized and its instrumentation technically unimpressive. In fact, its many parts have an accidental quality, as if one found oneself in a hall, halfway between two open doors, each releasing tones now mixing in the corridor. And yet the result is sometimes evocative, say between 2′30″ and 3′50″—a chance gathering of elements suggesting something more without indicating what that more is (▶ Audio 1.4).

An even greater density characterizes "2/2." An eight-second drone opens. From it, synthesizer tones rise with even less of a melodic character than what "1/1" and "2/1" offer. And the tones keep coming. None of the silences or spaces or solitary, ringing sustains that appeared on earlier tracks occur. Instead, a synthesizer resounds in pulses for over nine minutes. Some tones suggest ascents and descents, but others interrupt that movement, and nothing like a perceptible rhythm regulates the procession. Moreover, nothing like the expressive power of an instrument is being explored or celebrated. The synthesizer has been set to generate hornlike tones, but no one would wonder if a horn were being played. Rather, the attack of the notes, the way their envelope quickly opens and persists, is hornlike, but clearly produced in some other way.

More than the three preceding tracks, "2/2" is an arrangement of electronically generated sounds, and we seem invited to hear them as such. It thus intensifies the experiment with tape music that each of the other tracks pursue. But it does so in a rather discontinuous manner, which underscores that experiments are occurring. Because "1/2" combines short, improvisational piano phrases and ethereal voices, the third track might appear to develop musical patterns operative in "1/1" and "2/1." But "2/2" renders that line of listening implausible by focusing so intently on the comings and goings of sounds free of traditional Western musical orders (▶ Audio 1.5). *MFA* presents us with four tracks, not four movements articulating a whole larger than the sum of its parts. Nothing integral to the album would be lost, therefore, if one were to listen to the whole in different sequences.

What all of the tracks have in common is a concern for texture and relations freed from narrative development. The album shows an exquisite concern for the just-so qualities of the tones it arranges: the reverb of voices, the thunk of a keyboard, the juxtaposed feel of acoustic and electric pianos, the expanding mouth of tone after tone, the quaver of sounds fading away. And these textures change as one swaps one system of sound reproduction for another: a vinyl record, turntable, amplifier, and stereo speakers, or a CD player in your car, or an MP3, smartphone, and earbuds. That is, the textures that give *MFA* a good deal of its leading edge are not effects of Eno's compositional choices alone, but also of the ways in which listeners reproduce the recording. It would seem, then, that *MFA* is in part a product of multiple interactions, some of which arrive well after the album has been mastered.

With regard to Eno's work in general, Eric Tamm claims: "When so much in the way of melody, rhythm, and harmony have been stripped away from the music, timbral subtleties loom structurally large."[6] I find this mostly right and an essential thought to keep in mind when listening to *MFA*, though I wouldn't put it quite like that. It is less that melody, rhythm, and harmony have been stripped away than that they have been ignored in favor of other relations. (*MFA* abandons itself to the tones it gathers far more than it negates a musical tradition. As we will see, it moves in a space created by prior negations, but it avoids the horizon-wiping bravado of its avant-garde predecessors.) Moreover, I don't find the foregrounded textures "structural," if only because structure suggests something thereby structured. But *MFA*'s textures do not support some other facet of the work like a backbeat supports other parts of a pop song. Instead, the textures are genuinely surface phenomena—light, transitory. One catches them as one can. And when they prove evocative, the listener finds a hint but not the hinter or the hinted.

CHAPTER 2

MUSIC FOR AIRPORTS AND THE AVANT-GARDE

THE ACTIVITY OF SOUNDS

> New music: new listening. Not an attempt to understand something that is being said, for, if something were being said, the sound would be given the shapes of words. Just an attention to the activity of sounds.
>
> —John Cage, *Silence: Lectures and Writings*

After *Scary Monsters* (1980), the work of David Bowie became something of a junction. I wanted to listen to whoever else met there. Eno was an early encounter. Side two of Bowie's *Low* (1977) contains several captivating instrumentals. The first, "Warszawa," gives Eno a song credit, given that he is responsible for most everything but the vocals (though Tony Visconti's son is popularly credited with the initial piano sequence). The "song"—there is wordless singing in 4/4 time—slowly builds around a plaintive melody executed, organ-like, on an EMS Synthi, a cousin to the VCS 3 synthesizer that Eno used in Roxy

Music. In stark contrast to the two notes per measure allowed to ring (just out of sync) across the song's first eight measures, lengthy sustains become increasingly common as "Warszawa" unfolds. The result is rich in texture, which is what Bowie sought on that side of *Low*, and from Eno. Bowie felt he needed "textures, and of all the people that I've heard write textures, Brian's always appealed to me most."[1] (▶ Audio 2.1)

By 1983 I had heard my way through Eno's catalogue. The ambient albums stood out from what was then ten years of LPs, particularly *Discreet Music* (1975) and *Music for Airports*, alongside two albums with guitarist Robert Fripp, *(No Pussyfooting)* (1973) and *Evening Star* (1975). Thanks in part to liner notes and diagrams, I got it—Eno was manipulating sounds, letting them interact and marveling at some of the results, which he preserved. And I caught the sense that amateur ears were welcome. The sounds were the key, their activity, such as their attack and decay, their timbre, their duration (over which their timbre fluctuates, evidencing complexity within simplicity). But also how they interact, introducing new textures and intensities and affecting something like a mood. Moreover, the result that made its way onto the recording was just one possible result—their elements could have been combined in other ways. So, with two turntables, I started to play and mix LPs, recording the results onto cassette. The opening track of *Discreet Music* became a backdrop for "Swastika Girls" from *(No Pussyfooting)*. I also acquired two copies of *Evening Star* to play "Wind on Water" into "Wind on Wind" and back again, working with sections I favored and employing variable speeds.

The music was heady in one sense but ridiculously accessible in another. I wondered, was mixing also making music? The question was obvious. A convincing answer was not.

I recall this early experience because the history that follows is constructed for listeners who hear sounds as sounds but might know little about how this came to count as something like music. To this end, I have assembled a conceptual map that indicates a set of understandings that characterize what some regard as a sonic (or auditory) turn in the history of music, one that helps explain how a "new audio culture has emerged, a culture of musicians, composers, sound artists, scholars, and listeners attentive to sonic substance, the act of listening, and the creative possibilities of sound recording, playback, and transmission."[2] To be clear, I am not attributing discoveries or inventions to the particular persons I name. Nor am I offering a summary of their accomplishments or significance. Rather, I am explicating an aspect of a figure's work to draw a larger picture of the context out of which *MFA* emerged and to which it contributed.

In *Oceans of Sound*, David Toop, exploring the origins of ambient music, directs our attention to Claude Debussy (1862–1918), who sought "music entirely free from 'motifs,' or rather consisting of one continuous 'motif' which nothing interrupts and which never turns back on itself."[3] A motif, or motive, is a basic musical idea like the opening notes of Beethoven's Fifth Symphony, which is then developed as the piece progresses—that is, the piece turns back to a motif sounded earlier and repeats and varies it, perhaps developing it in new directions. And this, Toop suggests, is the approach that Debussy wished to abandon: building music around a set of core musical ideas.

Two points are salient for *MFA*. First, Debussy is making room for music that does not introduce a motif to develop it in various ways. Secondly, this calls for a new kind of listening. Without a motif to recall or its development to trace, how should we hear notes in their succession? Of course, Debussy's music remains broadly tonal, rhythmic, and harmonically rich, so we are not yet confronted by the activity of sounds as sounds. But a step toward "sound" has been made.

Another bend in the sonic turn finds Ferruccio Busoni (1886–1924), an Italian pianist known for his editions and transcriptions as well as his own compositions. Like the American composer Charles Ives (1874–1954), Busoni was interested in microtones, that is, the wealth of pitch differences that lie between the notes of the chromatic scale. As Busoni saw it, composition had been limited to the tones that acoustic instruments typically generate when tuned and played in a traditional manner. "Keyboard instruments in particular," he wrote of Western equal temperament, the division of the octave into twelve equal tones, "have so thoroughly schooled our ears that we are no longer capable of hearing anything else—incapable of hearing except through this impure medium. Yet Nature created an *infinite gradation—infinite!* who knows it nowadays?"[4]

Busoni's lament is as important for its longing as for its negation. On the one hand, it suggests that very traditional musical means—standard pitches and instruments—have artificially, even unnaturally, dulled us to genuine musical possibilities, and, more broadly, to nature writ large.

And this in turn calls for the production of new tunings or instruments able to access what current technologies precluded. (The sustained synthesizer drones across *MFA* are in line with this development.) But it also calls upon listeners to remain receptive to what usually accompanies the introduction of microtones into standard tonal music: dissonance beyond what the chromatic scale provides, as Ives's *Three Quarter-Tone Pieces* (1924) makes plain (Audio 2.2).

By asking us to compose (and listen) in a manner unchained to motifs and the pitches registered by the chromatic scale, Debussy and Busoni created room for new sounds and sound organizations. In an effort to emancipate dissonance, Arnold Schoenberg (1874–1951) also contributed to this expansion. Harmony names the relation between the notes of a single chord as well as between successive chords. In traditional Western music, harmonic relations are experienced as balanced and fitting. Over extended chord progressions, moving away from and returning to the tonic (or tonal center of the scale) maintains balance (and interest) in a more general sense. Movement away from the tonic builds tensions and may be heard as dissonance, whereas returns have the character of consonance and resolution. Schoenberg argued that consonance and dissonance are not opposites; rather, they are names for qualitatively different relations between all the tones in the chromatic scale.

Traditional harmonic structures provide a map for composers and listeners alike, prescribing various relations among pitches and chord progressions played simultaneously. If no single relation among pitches and chords is considered any more or less "harmonic" than any other, then the number of possible combinations increases significantly, as you can hear across Schoenberg's *Six Little Piano Pieces* (1911). To be sure, Schoenberg is less abandoning than expanding the traditional conception of harmony, which, according to a note of his of October 1936, "fulfills structural purposes; that is to say, it is the framework and, indeed, probably the blueprint of every musical edifice," including those found in "music free of tonality."[5] And that marks a concern that seems completely absent from *Music for Airports*, as the printed "scores" indicate. But like Busoni, Schoenberg forced the musical world to imagine new ways in which tones might combine in a manner whose integrity we should labor to hear.

If Schoenberg imagined new harmonic possibilities in the dissonances of traditional European composition and performance, a few Italian artists looked for new harmonic and rhythmic possibilities in the emerging soundscapes of modern life.[6] Writing in 1913, Luigi Russolo added a startling thought to a familiar complaint. "Musical sound . . . is too limited in its qualitative variety of timbres," he wrote, insisting: "We must break out of this restricted circle of pure sounds and conquer the infinite variety of noise-sounds."[7] Noise-sounds? Thunder and wind, animals, vehicles in motion, even "the white breath of a city at night."[8] Because it opens every sound to composition (not just dissonant tones and microtones), Russolo's position marks a significant turn of musical thought, one that makes room for *MFA*'s relatively simple musical gestures. All sounds count. The challenge now lies in arranging and presenting them in interesting ways. Moreover, such a capacious sense of sound also required instruments able to make and work with these sounds—to "conquer" them. Russolo thus constructed *intonarumori*, "noise intoners," to simulate the sonic character or sonority of classes of sounds like whistles or screeches.[9]

Russolo's composition *Awakening of a City* (1914) enacts his program. For example, the opening twenty-five or so seconds call to mind a machine kicking into gear, its increasing rotations indicated by the ascending pitches and the resolution of the tones into a unified whir after twenty seconds (▶ Audio 2.3). The somewhat extended silences (for example, 0′26″–0′30″), also indicate that a city awakens differently at different points. Because the *intonarumori* are limited in the range of sounds they can generate, "Awakening of a City" is somewhat limited as a piece of program music—and, as program music, it is quite different than *MFA*. But it exemplifies a clear expansion in the range of sounds open to one purporting to compose music, and it indicates how technological innovation is part and parcel of the process.

Russolo's program requires the discovery of sonic analogues for the music awaiting us in the field of noise, analogues that can in turn be composed and performed. The *musique concrète* of Pierre Schaefer (1910–95) radicalized that project. Empowered by technological advances that allowed him to record and manipulate found sounds, Schaeffer, a radio engineer with philosophical sophistication, sought to develop a "discrete and complete sound object," one tied neither to traditional instruments nor to a recognizable source. Instead, manipulation would release "sound in its native state," which could then function as a

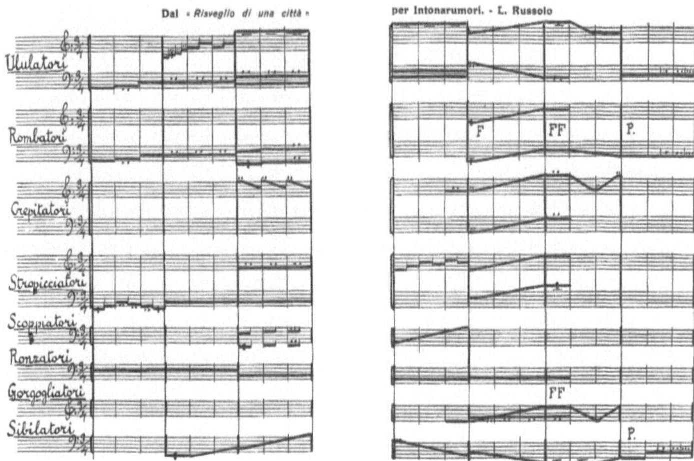

FIGURE 2.1 A page from the score for *Awakening of a City*

"musical element that was pure, composable, and had an original timbre."[10]

Schaeffer's preoccupation with "sound in its native state" strikes me as decisive for an album like *MFA*. The task of the composer is to hear *and* arrange sounds according to something like their own character, and to arrange them in a manner that recognizes and resonates with that character. While Eno does not share Schaeffer's goal of first freeing and articulating a "discrete and complete sound object" from the experiential field of found sounds (say, airport sounds), *MFA* remains an heir of *musique concrète* insofar as the latter frees itself to work with sounds more or less outside traditional Western musical structures, including dissonant, atonal, or polytonal registers. (Listen to Schaeffer's *Etude aux chemins de fer*, which offers a progression of tones drawn from trains that celebrates the dynamics and timbre of the trains.) (▶ Audio 2.4)

Schaeffer's approach raises a vital question in the sonic turn. How does one genuinely attend to the activity of sounds? Is that activity immediately available? Or must it be freed from what we initially hear, as Schaeffer believed? Or is the question of veracity even pertinent? Even a brief review of the sonic turn encounters a diversity of goals operating among those who brought it about. Some composers have aesthetic goals, such as increased materials for beautiful works (Debussy). Others seek new expressions for a newly emerging humanity. Francesco Pratella, to whom Russolo's *The Art of Noises* is dedicated, wrote: "Sky, water, forests, . . . criss-crossing ships and swarming cities are transformed by the soul of the musician into marvelous and potent voices that sing with human tones the desires of man."[11] Schaeffer, in contrast, has what we might term epistemic goals; he seeks a music that discovers and presents something like the activity of sounds. But that activity must be wrested from what we normally hear.

I don't want to make too much of these categories for compositional goals. They are somewhat vague, and my assignments overly simple. But in a general way, they invoke something essential. The composers of the sonic turn have different aims, and those aims inform how each understands (a) the "activity of sounds," and (b) what is achieved when one begins to hear it—say, beauty without motifs, the drama of the human spirit in the age of machines, or nature resounding behind the obscuring veil of traditional music. Setting *MFA* within the sonic turn not only renders its sonic character more salient. It leads us to ask: How should we understand the character of the sounds it organizes and their relation to those situations in which they are produced and played? (The chapters that address *MFA* as ambient music and conceptual art will offer partial replies.)

In mapping the sonic turn through shifting concepts and goals, I do not mean to underplay the contributions of technological development, which often enabled compositional innovations.[12] The work of Edgard Varèse (1883–1965) exemplifies this interaction. Already in the 1920s Varèse "decided to call [his] music 'organized sound' and [himself] not a musician, but 'a worker in rhythms, frequencies, and intensities.' "[13] Initially, this led to works that combined conventional and non-conventional instruments—for example, *Amériques* (1929), which adds sirens to common orchestral instruments. But Varèse repeatedly embraced new electronic sound technologies, seeking better ways to execute his program. He celebrated the electronic because, as he wrote, "It has freed music from the tempered system, it has made a wealth of new sounds available, and it has made possible the simultaneity of unrelated elements."[14]

Varèse's threefold enthusiasm for electronic music echoes across *MFA*. Varèse is interested not only in rendering musical the sounds of the world, but in generating new sounds with which to compose. (If the issue is sound, why restrict the field? This is the kind of question one can imagine Varèse and Eno posing.) Second, having sounds at one's disposal, that is, recorded and manipulable in ways that can also be recorded, allows one to experiment with various combinations based on how they sound, even if they were initially generated by traditional instruments, like the two pianos on "1/1." One can begin to play with sounds as sounds (as sound material) rather than with notes or chords. And one can play with notes and chords as sound material, dislocating them from their place in the chromatic scale and its manifold harmonic orders. (As if anticipating the rectangular shades that Eno uses to visualize "1/2," Varèse talks about the "movement of sound masses, of shifting planes," which interact in "Zones of Intensities.")[15]

Varèse's *Poème Electronique* (1957–58) provides a sense of how electronics expand the field of sonic possibilities. Composed in response to an invitation from the architect Le Corbusier (1887–1965), the work used several hundred playback speakers (and multiple amplifiers) as its

FIGURE 2.2 Varèse listening to *Poème Electronique*

orchestra, and it had its first performance at the Brussels World's Fair in 1958 in a pavilion designed by Le Corbusier and the composer Iannis Xenakis just for the occasion. The work is thoroughly composed of electronically recorded and reproduced sounds, which, across eight or so minutes, crescendo in a machine-like whirr. At various points one hears a tolling bell, non-referential buzzes and squeaks, sine waves, bongos, a human voice, and so forth. And most if not all are manipulated; for example, their pitch is adjusted (0′20″–0′24″ and 7′38″–7′58″), so that they rise and fall without any break, thus obscuring the difference between tones and microtones. Or buzzes are "panned" (0′32″–0′38″), moving across the sound field created by the speakers. (The piece was thus composed on electronics for electronics.) Others are subjected to an echo effect as well as pitch control, which gives the voice between 3′39″ and 4′15″ a ghostly texture. And texture (and dynamics) is very much foregrounded, as with the building drone, which unfolds between 3′12″ and 3′24″. As an odd inheritor of the tone poem tradition, *Poème Electronique* dramatizes the character of numerous sounds as they change with shifts in duration, pitch, juxtaposition, placement in a stereophonic field, and so on (▶ Audio 2.5).

Something startling becomes possible once we agree that the manipulation of electronic sound sources results in music. One only needs to know how to work the electronics in order to produce a piece. One doesn't need to know music theory or even how to play a traditional instrument. It would seem, then, as Richard Taruskin observes, that electronic music enables the emergence of a "post-literate musical culture."[16] Not that one can seize this possibility without skill or judgment. But the resulting music need not and probably does not revolve around traditional Western musical notation. It should be no surprise, therefore, that *MFA* does without a traditional score, and that Eno underscores the fact with something quite different. As he told Jim Aikin in 1981: "Let's say I know many theories about music, but I don't know that particular one that has to do with notation."[17]

John Cage (1912–92) also sought to rethink music as the "organization of sound," and already in 1937 he saw that electrical sources and reproduction systems would lead the way.[18] But he did so in a particularly radical manner, denying that any sound was somehow, in principle, non-musical. His work not only produces and arranges a whole host of seeming noise, it also makes sounds at the expense of traditional instruments, such as by having the performer play the piano with the keyboard cover closed, as with "The Wonderful Widow of Eighteen Strings" (1942). Moreover, unlike most of his avant-garde predecessors, Cage sought to minimize if not erase the composer's contribution to the final result, thereby allowing each performance to give pieces a new organization and sonic character, thus breaking with the idea that the composer completes the work. As Michael Nyman has chronicled, this opened a path for experimental composers who "are by and large not concerned with prescribing a defined *time-object* whose materials, structuring, and relationships are calculated and arranged in advance," such as we have with *Poème Electronique*, "but are more excited by the prospect of outlining *a situation* in which sounds may occur."[19]

FIGURE 2.3 John Cage in 1966. Photo © Hulton-Deutsch Collection/CORBIS/Corbis via Getty Images.

While Cage's place in the sonic turn is central, two facets of his experimental orientation are particularly crucial for *MFA*. In his experimental compositions, Cage blurs the distinction between the sounds of the world and those of the work, much as *MFA* does when it provides a "tint" or "atmosphere," which, Eno claims, is its aim as an ambient work. Drawing inspiration from Satie's "musical furnishings," and as a clear precedent to *MFA*, Cage's music tries to join the world rather than replace it for the time being.

Nothing better concretizes this thought than Cage's infamous *4′33″* (1952), in which a performer or group of performers present an instrument or instruments and refrains from playing—the instruction is to remain silent. (At the premier, David Tudor, sitting before a piano, closed and opened the piano to indicate the beginning and ending of three distinct movements. But that gesture was not scored as a way of playing the piano.) Conceptually, the piece demonstrates that there is never silence, only unintended sounds. But in the tradition of other proponents of the sonic turn, *4′33″* also directs listeners to sounds that it cannot help but frame in a temporal way, and it presses one to give them the same attention one would normally give the piano. As Cage has it, there is music, or better still, sounds worthy of our attention, all the way down (and around).

Cage not only embraced chance and indeterminacy over the course of a performance, however. To better let sounds be sounds, Cage strove, almost paradoxically, to build pieces from unintended sound sources. *MFA* follows suit. "I just set all of these loops running," Eno says of creating the work, "and let them configure in whichever way they wanted."[20] While Eno first encountered this procedure in the early tape works of Steve Reich (b. 1936), the basic thought is already operative in Cage's compositions. *Imaginary Landscape no. 4* (1951) involves twelve radios, which shows Cage replacing the chromatic scale with new musical sources (▶ Audio 2.6). One performer manipulates the volume, another the dial, each according to directions scored by Cage. The work is experimental—whatever is on the radio at a given frequency provides sound material for the composition. The work is also perpetually singular. Different locations and times will lead to different stations and programming and thus to a different work. "It is thus possible," Cage wrote, reflecting on the piece, "to make a musical composition the continuity of which is free of individual taste and memory (psychology) and also of literature and 'traditions' of art."[21]

A few twists remain in my recounting. In works like "I Am Sitting in a Room" (1969), Alvin Lucier (b. 1931) elected to play the sound of a room rather than simply frame the sounds therein. "Every room has its own melody," he writes, "hiding there until it is made audible."[22] The key is to fill a room with sound until the resonant frequencies of the room reinforce themselves and remain while other frequencies disappear. "I Am Sitting in a Room" accomplishes this by amplifying a spoken passage, recording it, playing it back and recording it again with the room's natural reverb in tow, and then recording that iteration, playing it back, recording it, and so forth, until one more or less hears the room as a "resonant environment." Lucier's work is significant because it highlights another facet of the activity of sounds, namely, the contribution made by the resonant environments in which they are generated. And with a work like *MFA* in view, it helps us listen for the contributions made by the various resonant environments in play whenever the album is played or the work performed, including loudspeakers and earbuds (▶ Audio 2.7).

La Monte Young (b. 1935) and Terry Riley (b. 1935) close this necessarily incomplete tale. (In later discussions, we'll return to some of these figures, particularly Satie and Reich.) In "Lecture 1960," Young accords each sound "its own world" and announces: "I like to get inside of a sound." Furthermore, and echoing Cage, he claims that the "trouble with most music of the past is that man has tried to make the sounds do what he wants them to do," and he suggests that "we should allow the sounds to be sounds instead of trying to force them to do things that are mainly pertinent to human existence."[23] A piece from the same year, *Compositions 1960: #7*, executes the thought. The score, just one measure in length, calls for the simultaneous

FIGURE 2.4 Alvin Lucier. Photo by Amanda Lucier.

production of a B and an F♯, with the instruction "To be held for a long time." No instrument is specified. The task, I think, is to hear complexity in what might seem to be a simple dyad, typically just a part to be used in the construction of a larger musical structure. As the two pitches ring, and this becomes even more apparent when *#7* is played on an amplified electric guitar, small fluctuations in tone and emergent overtones appear and establish a field of relations immanent to, rather than imposed upon, the sound. To be clear, the point is not simply conceptual. *Compositions 1960: #7* offers a pair of tones that should absorb their listeners, which is why Young was able to expand his efforts, experimenting with sustained tones (or drones), as he did in *The Second Dream of the High-Tension Line Stepdown Transformer* (1962). That work involves repeatedly producing and sustaining four pitches, C, F, F♯, and G, for varying lengths of time, surrounded by rests instituted to give each pitch and pitch combination sufficient breathing room.

There is a kind seeming purity to Young's ear for sound. And his use of lengthy sustains to expose the complexity of tones is a clear predecessor to the longer tones one finds in *MFA*, as is Young's judicious use of rests. Also, Young's feel for the complexity of single tones underwrites *MFA*'s embrace of simple sounds. But like Busoni and Schoenberg before him, a deeper concern drives Young's compositions—exposing and articulating harmonic orders, or what Young regards as vibrations, which he describes as "rhythm on a much higher level."[24] (Speaking of *The Second Dream*, which hums like a transformer on a telephone pole, Young insists one "can find the 17th harmonic up there and put it in the range of 12, 16, 17, and 18.")[25]

Young found more than mere music in these harmonies. He came to regard his compositions and performances as religious rituals designed to reconnect those in attendance to core cosmic processes. As Jeremy Grimshaw observes: "By reducing music to its most elementary nature, sustained vibration, Young has sought to reveal its connection to the periodicities of the earth around him and the universe around it."[26] Cage too regarded his liberation of noise as spiritual in intent and effect. But his commitment to Zen led him to abandon the thought that any order or reality lies behind things in their fleeting appearance. Young, however, driven by his Mormon upbringing and studies in Indian music and spirituality, has never ceased thinking that each appearance, musical or otherwise, indicates, however obscurely, an enveloping order of vibrations lost to the habits and obsessions of everyday life. (As we'll see in chapter 5, *MFA* has its own point of view on these matters.)

Young had a profound effect on Terry Riley, whose early work took the sonic turn in an unexpected direction decisive for *MFA*. Riley did not abandon consonance, and this distinguishes him from most of the figures we've discussed. His most famous work, *In C* (1964), unfolds mostly in C major, a key almost prudishly avoided by most avant-garde composers. But we'll lose the point if we make it this way, particularly since Riley is more interested in working with vibrations and their cosmic import than with keys and their historical significance. The more basic issue is accessibility. Riley's compositions are easy to follow at an intuitive level—they make sense to an untutored ear. One can follow the consistent eight note pulse, kept, for example, by a xylophone on the twenty-fifth anniversary concert recording (foot tapping allowed, in other words). (▶ Audio 2.8) One also quickly catches the introduction of new parts, which always arise smoothly out of their predecessors. Under Riley's direction, therefore, avant-garde techniques entered frankly hummable music, and this brought the sonic turn into non-academic arenas, which helped create a context wherein a sometimes rock persona might venture an album like *MFA*—a stretch for many ears, but not an unthinkable one.

All histories bear the marks of their telling. If I hadn't organized mine around Eno's education and experiences, this brief history of the sonic turn could have looked and sounded different. One could, for example, enter the sonic turn through conceptions of community underwriting compositional techniques and/or performance practices. This would underscore social interactions within the generation of sound (as with *In C*) and open a door to other musicians, such as the Roscoe Mitchell Sextet and their LP *Sound* (1966). Through the disciplined but transgressive exercise of traditional instruments and musical sources such as the alto saxophone as well as Dixieland, the album finds new approaches to and enactments of "sound." Moreover, these reconstructions also enact a "communal sensitivity" that Ronald Radano finds coursing through the Chicago scene to which Mitchell belongs—"they built 'community' into the art itself."[27] But in a short book, one is forced to make choices, and I elected to provide what I consider *MFA*'s most immediate context, which does not seem to include work like *Sound*.

Histories also can suggest that what they track lies in the past. But the sonic turn continues to unfold. New sound material has been found and composed, such as microsounds, accessed and assembled through computer manipulations of digital files. Composers have also focused on volume, some favoring the quiet to inaudible, others loud assaults, each offering novel sonic experiences.[28] But my goal has not been to fully or even partially account for the sonic turn. Rather, I've been marking conceptual, technological, and sonic shifts that helped make a record like *MFA* possible, and we've encountered several.

- Music can be built around something other than a motif, or basic musical phrase.

- Microtones and the dissonances they introduce can be musical.
- Traditional harmony (and even harmony altogether) neither exhausts nor is required for a musically legitimate arrangement of sounds.
- Any sound is suitable material for a musical composition.
- New technologies for the generation and reproduction of sounds are not only welcome but also necessary.
- The presence of unintended sounds, i.e., noise, is an acceptable (and inevitable) part of a musical work.
- Musical works can productively interact with the sonic environment in which they are produced.
- Single tones and chords are musically complex and interesting, particularly when sustained for lengthy periods of time or subjected to extended repetition.

All of these positions helped secure a listening space for *MFA*, which not only stands as their heir and compatriot. It too pursues sounds in ways that ask us to listen in nontraditional ways. Moreover, the shifts evident in these conceptualizations generate the beginnings of a vocabulary for what *MFA* offers listeners: *the activity of sounds*, *organized sound*, and *sound masses* with their *zones of intensity*. And given the various purposes propelling these shifts, whether an expanded palette for beauty or a search for spiritually significant vibrations, we know that "the activity of sounds" can indicate very different phenomena. But before we further consider what orients *MFA*, let's explore how a rock star found his way into the musical avant-garde.

CHAPTER 3

ENO'S JOURNEY FROM ART SCHOOL TO THE STUDIO

BECOMING A NON-MUSICIAN

I am an anti-musician.

—Eno, in "Eno: Non-Musician on Non-Art"

At times, Eno has presented himself as a non-musician, even an anti-musician, as the epigraph states. In an article from 1973, Nick Kent, writing for *New Musical Express*, refers to "the man who has already been described in the press as a 'self-confessed musical illiterate.'"[1] And in 1980, speaking with Cage, Eno noted: "Writing music is so far from anything I'm capable of doing, it's a very foreign form to me."[2] But instead of setting Eno outside of music, these remarks indicate how Eno belongs to music; they locate him within a field of musical activities by distancing him from the usual agent of those activities, the musician.

FIGURE 3.1 John Cage and Brian Eno. Photo by Michael Putland/Getty Images.

In his explanation of himself to Jim Aikin, Eno's notion of being a non-musician evidences three dimensions.[3] The first concerns musical notation and theories like harmony that explore the phenomena mapped by notation, like pitches and chords. Eno doesn't read music, or at least not easily. But even more than that (to draw from an interview given two years prior), he doesn't compose by assembling sounds according to notated patterns. "The things I think about mostly when I'm recording now don't seem to be musical considerations at all . . . more like descriptive thoughts . . . an aural picture."[4] Think back to "1/2." Its floating "ahhhhhs" were recorded to tape while Eno was in Germany. They were later manipulated, set into sub-tracks, and copied to another tape. They recur in extended patterns that do not repeat over the course of the track but cluster and interact in zones of varying intensity. Because he did not prepare a notated score for the performers whose enactment he recorded, Eno's "non-musician" stance seems almost conscientious. He is working in a widening stream of post-literate musical culture.

Notation (and its theory) does not complete the story, however. Eno also does not aspire to virtuosity. "I have pretty perfect pitch," he states, but he confesses to only knowing how to do simple things with the basic instruments of rock music: guitars, basses, and keyboards.[5] He is thus not a musician in the sense of a trained or virtuoso performer. But that is because he approaches instruments for their ability to generate sounds. This is why he sometimes refers to instruments with odd qualifiers like "snake guitar," as he does on the album *Another Green World* (where he also refers to "desert guitars"). You can hear it across the opening track, "Sky Saw," a slurred (or slithering) four-"note" line (▶ Audio 3.1). When asked by Lester Bangs about these qualifiers, Eno replied: "All those words are my descriptions of either a way of playing or a sound; in that case [snake guitar] it was because the kind of lines I was playing reminded me of the way a snake moves through the brush, a sort of speedy, forceful, liquid quality."[6] And several years earlier, referring to a Mike Oldfield solo on Kevin Ayer's *Songs from the Bottom of the Well*, Eno also stressed the "non-musician" undertones of the concept. "Snake guitar requires no particular skill," he wrote, "and essentially involves *destroying the pitch element of the instrument* in order to produce wedges of sound that can be used percussively or as a kind of punctuation."[7]

One other variable is in play. As a producer, and one often interested in generating soundscapes, Eno does not have (nor has he sought) advanced knowledge of psychoacoustics. *MFA* was made to spread through and work with various locales and situations, but not by knowing the acoustics of any space or the psychoacoustics of average listeners. Instead, Eno found his way with something like aesthetic judgment. "Most of my research in that area," he tells Aikin, "has been fairly intuitive, or based on a study of my own reaction to things."[8]

In the areas of music theory, performance, and production, the non-musician eschews technical knowledge. In their place, two other orientations operate: (1) an intuitive sense of what sounds good and, crucially, (2) a highly reflexive approach to the generation and arrangement of sounds as well as to the activity of the artist. Recall a remark quoted in the last chapter. When told "You don't know music theory and things of that sort," his reply was quite careful. "No, I don't. Well, let's say I know many theories about music, but I don't know that particular one that has to do with notation."[9] This is the key. The technical is abandoned in favor of a theoretical space within which sounds can be organized, say by way of repetition, error, and echo, operations whose realization do not require the presence of "musicians." When I hear "non-musician," therefore, I think less about certain facts (he can't read music, he can't really play anything, he can't . . .) and more about the sensibility with which Eno operates: (a) minimal to modest technique (but no virtuosity), (b) self-trust in intuitive judgments, and (c) a willingness to let more general theories (as opposed to music theory) propel his creative efforts.

But how does one become a non-musician, and how, in particular, did Eno find himself making albums that aspire to the condition of painting? Eno's path is sufficiently fascinating to merit a brief recounting, with a focus on circumstances and events that allowed him to craft *MFA*.[10]

Eno was born May 15, 1948, in Woodbridge, Suffolk, seventy-five miles or so from London. David Shepherd describes Woodbridge as a "place of seclusion, ancient history, and patrician charm" that nevertheless had room for several eccentrics.[11] Raised Catholic, Eno developed a feel (and love) for hymns and their sonorities. Two nearby US army bases also gave him access to early rock 'n' roll, with doo-wop a particular interest. While he managed a brief stint drumming for a local group, the Black Aces, access to numerous keyboard parts owned by his grandfather, who repaired keyboards for a living, oriented Eno toward gadgets and, more importantly, the realization that anything that makes a sound can be sounded in unconventional ways. As Shepherd reports, he once added holes to player piano scrolls, thereby transforming their end results.[12]

In 1964, Eno began studying visual art at Ipswich Civic College, though less with the hope of becoming a painter than a the sense that he didn't want a job.[13] Through a teacher of his, painter Tom Philips (b. 1937), he encountered Cage and was introduced to Britain's avant-garde music scene. Philips also reinforced Eno's pursuit of rigor, or what Philips terms "probity, to do things properly, with a kind of dedication that doesn't allow you to fudge."[14] But the overarching curriculum, animated by Roy Ascott (b. 1934), also impacted Eno's development. "What he and his staff were concerned with was not the teaching of technique so much

FIGURE 3.2 Tom Phillips in 2008. Photo: Lucy Shortis.

as experimenting with notions of what constitutes creative behavior."[15]

Ascott brought a cybernetic conception to art. Derived from the theories of Norbert Wiener (1894–1964), cybernetics focuses upon the logic of systems and their impact upon those who work within them. According to Ascott, art is a complex network of interactions among subsystems (principally artist-work-audience) whose behavior is complex in ways that traditional art education overlooks in its focus on technique. "The artist, the artifact, and the spectator," Ascott writes, "are all involved in a more behavioral context."[16] Ascott thus required students to think of their art as engagements with audiences in open-ended processes built

FIGURE 3.3 Roy Ascott

around (rather than objectified by) the work. And while an artist initiates the process, she or he does not and cannot control the outcome.[17]

The conceptual shifts prompted by Ascott's pedagogy prepared the way for Eno the anti-musician. The move away from technique rendered virtuosity inessential, even shortsighted. An ability to account for one's intervention in an art situation was valorized instead, an intervention that, in the absence of technique, often took its leave from inspiration or intuition. "Ipswich made me become fascinated in the connection between the intellect and intuition. Normally these things are seen as disconnected; but I came out thinking that they were part of a continuum."[18] And that continuum also flowed from painting to music. "It wasn't a big move from art to music," Eno notes, "because there is a strong link between them in that both concentrate on systems—as far as I am concerned, anyway. I had reached a stage in painting where I was actually making a score which I would then carry out in the same way that a musician might."[19] It seems, therefore, that while Eno's music, particularly *MFA*, is painterly, his own paintings tended to derive from instructions for dynamic interactions (which is one way to regard musical scores). One example involved asking one artist to paint and hide a painting and another to reconstruct it from whatever clues were left in the studio where it was created, such as paint drips and testimonials from those who had seen the original.[20] When the reproduction was considered complete—by the second painter—both would be hung together.

While studying at Ipswich introduced Eno to avant-garde music and provided him with a sensibility that would inform many of his later musical practices, his work with music intensified at Winchester College of Art, where he began a three-year program in 1966. Elected to run the student union, he proceeded to bring the avant-garde to campus, including Morton Feldman (1926–87) and Christian Wolff (b. 1934), both students of Cage, as well as Cornelius Cardew (1936–81), who spearheaded Britain's avant-garde efforts.[21] Eno began performing as well, including a composition by Young, *arabic numeral (any integer)*, which is also known as *X for Henry Flynt* (1960). As Young recalls, the piece "consists of some number of forearm clusters on a piano keyboard or strokes on a gong. The integer represents the number of strokes."[22] Young's piece falls right in line with the kind of approach favored at Ipswich—the artwork is a set of instructions to be executed rather than a finished artifact. Eno performed the piece twice, once with outstretched arms for sixty minutes, another time with flat piece of wood for ninety. Whereas the repetition intrigued Young, Eno was also intrigued by what distinguished each stroke: "Sometimes you don't get a white down properly or miss a black, and just missing one note out of the fifty or so you're covering is a very noticeable difference, you really can hear it."[23] And over time, it is the differences that draw one's attention, as well as the acoustics of the room, Lucier's "resonant environments." Eno found that fascinating, even hallucinatory, though limiting as well. "Part of the thrill from something like that is that from such an economical source so much happens. Once you know that, there isn't that thrill anymore; you sit down to another of those pieces of unchanging music and think, 'Oh well, I know what's gonna happen now.' "[24]

In accounting for Eno's development, one shouldn't make too much of any single event. But aspects of Eno's performance and experience of Young's *integer* seem decisive for *MFA*. Of Young's work, Eno has said: "This was the first piece of music I ever performed from a score—and the first piece that, having performed, I felt really convinced that I'd made music."[25] With *integer*, Eno worked with organized sound rather than a music score, and in a very avant-garde manner. In a way, then, he was already something of an anti-musician before he even entered the rock world.[26] Second, the dynamic of "variety in repetition" is the work's decisive feature as Eno recalls it, and it resounds across MFA, albeit in a modified manner. Each track stays true to Eno's sense that the thrill of strict repetition fades rather quickly. What holds one's interest, however (at least

Eno's and mine) and what organizes *MFA* are approximations that recall rather than repeat each other without unfolding a melody—it "constantly changes but never really goes anywhere." Listen again to the first three piano phrases in "1/1": 0′2″–0′12″, 0′25″–0′40″, 0′47″–1′17″ (▶ Audio 3.2). While the third occurs again between 2′17″–2′46″, the first and second do not, and the recurrence of the longer phrase is also surrounded by different sounds the second time around. The effect is thus quite unlike *integer.* Strict or even adequate repetition—defined by the effort to do the same thing again—tends to fade from view over time, to be replaced by whatever differences can be found. Eno's recurring approximations—defined by the aim to enact what is similar but perceptibly not the same—linger as we listen, maintaining (or preserving) more continuity between the full range of sounds involved.

In the meantime, Eno remained in contact with Philips, his teacher from Ipswich, and through him encountered the Scratch Orchestra, whose principal leader was Cardew. In the early 1960s, Cardew looked on scores as instructions for performers rather than graphic representations of musical orders that performers should carry out. For him, music was first and foremost a social interaction, and his own scores were designed to initiate it.[27] But not just any kind of interaction; Cardew was a Maoist whose egalitarian commitments led him to welcome amateurs like Eno, including those without musical training of any kind, and in a context of extended group performances that might simulate and stimulate collective action.

Eno's brief time with the Scratch Orchestra also complemented his experiences performing Young's *integer.*

Cardew's massive *Great Learning* (1968–71) scored seven texts from a Confucian classic of the same name. While performing the last text, "Paragraph 7," (which appeared in 1971 on a Deutsche Grammophon LP, alongside "Paragraph 2"), Eno witnessed how simple instructions led not only to diverse, unpredictable results but also to moments of unscripted order, even "organic richness," to use Eno's own language.[28]

"Paragraph 7," as the score shows, involves twenty-five vocal parts scored without notation. Each part concerns a different word or phrase from the text, and each singer should sing each part. (The score does not call for a specific number of singers.) The pitch of the first part is left to the discretion of the singers, who enter together and sing "If" eight times, holding each note for the length of a breath (which will vary with each performer). On the remaining lines, however, some direction is given. Each singer should sing a note they hear being sung by another unless one of two conditions apply: (a) the singer is unable to hit the note(s) heard, or, (b) all the notes heard are identical to whatever they are singing/just sang (no repeats allowed). If either (a) or (b) applies, the singer may again choose freely.

When enacted, something approaching unison obtains. In being required to sing what they hear others singing, parts should fall in line with one another. But not completely. Variety among voices, even in the same register (bass, baritone, alto, etc.) as well as different backgrounds and levels of training on the part of the singers will inevitably bring textures and shadings to even those parts singing the same note. And because singers are prohibited from

Cornelius Cardew (1931-1981), *The Great Learning*, Paragraph 7
- SCORE -

------>	sing 8	IF
	sing 5	THE ROOT
	sing 13 (f3)	BE IN CONFUSION
	sing 6	NOTHING
	sing 5 (f1)	WILL
	sing 8	BE
	sing 8	WELL
	sing 7	GOVERNED
	hum 7	
------>	sing 8	THE SOLID
	sing 8	CANNOT BE
	sing 9 (f2)	SWEPT AWAY
	sing 8	AS
	sing 17 (f1)	TRIVIAL
	sing 6	AND
	sing 8	NOR
	sing 8	CAN
	sing 17 (f1)	TRASH
	sing 8	BE ESTABLISHED AS
	sing 9 (f2)	SOLID
	sing 5 (f1)	IT JUST
	sing 4	DOES NOT
	sing 6 (f1)	HAPPEN
	hum 3 (f2)	
------>	speak 1	MISTAKE NOT CLIFF FOR MORASS AND TREACHEROUS BRAMBLE

NOTATION

-----> The leader gives a signal and all enter concertedly at the same moment. The second of these signals is optional; those wishing to observe it should gather to the leader and choose a new note and enter just as at the beginning (see below).

FIGURE 3.4 The score to "Paragraph 7" of Cardew's *Great Learning*. Used with the permission of Horace Cardew.

"Sing 9 (f2) SWEPT AWAY" means: sing the words "SWEPT AWAY" on a length-of-a-breath note (syllables freely disposed) nine times; the same note each time; of the nine notes two (any two) should be loud, the rest soft. After each note take in breath and sing again.

"Hum 7" means: hum a length-of-a-breath note seven times; the same note each time; all soft.

"Speak 1" means: speak the given words in steady tempo all together, in a low voice, once (follow the leader).

PROCEDURE

Each chorus member chooses his or her own note (silently) for the first line ("IF" eight times). All enter together on the leader's signal. For each subsequent line choose a note that you can hear being sung by a colleague. It may be necessary to move to within earshot of certain notes. The note, once chosen, must be carefully retained. Time may be taken over the choice. If there is no note, or only the note you have just been singing, or only a note or notes that you are unable to sing, choose your note for the next line freely. Do not sing the same note on two consecutive lines.

Each singer progresses through the text at his own speed. Remain stationary for the duration of a line; move around only between lines.

All must have completed "hum 3 (f2)" before the signal for the last line is given. At the leader's discretion this last line may be omitted.

FIGURE 3.4 Continued

singing the same note two lines in a row, new tones should enter and spread.

Eno performed "Paragraph 7" several times, and it seems to have had a real impact upon his own approach to music. His 1976 essay, "Generating and Organizing Variety in the Arts," which is something of a manifesto, devotes sixteen of its twenty-five paragraphs to "Paragraph 7."[29] Moreover, "Paragraph 7" enabled Eno to construct a continuum (or "scale of orientations") along which his own work can be situated. At one end, Eno finds scores that know where they want to go. Through notation, they instruct performers to play particular instruments according to particular patterns. And while interpretation is inevitable in performance, the result is usually unsurprising. At the other end lies completely free improvisation—players responding to players playing without any score or even a riff on hand. A step or two in from that extreme fall pieces like "Paragraph 7." General instructions or rules are introduced, as well as a text, but they underspecify key actions—for example, which note to sing and exactly how long to hold it. And that leads to unexpected, unpredictable results—what Eno regards as "variety."

MFA is very much a child of "Paragraph 7" and other "systems music" of the time. Its asynchronous deployment of subtracks produces novel results over the course of the piece. Eno described this process regarding "2/1," looking back from 1996. "So as the piece progresses," he says, "what you hear are the various clusterings and configurations of these six basic elements [vocal tracks, "ahhhhhs"]. The basic elements in that particular piece never change. . . . But the piece does appear to have a lot of variety."[30]

As tape music, however, *MFA*'s "scores" are visual descriptions rather than instructions for performers. The album's ability to generate variety therefore cannot rely on the spontaneous choices and adjustments of people singing together. (It also cannot have the same political import of Cardew's piece, which allows people to act as individuals and community members simultaneously, and in a way that requires spontaneous responsiveness for the duration of the piece.)

Luckily for Eno, some of Steve Reich's early tape works, particularly *It's Gonna Rain* (1965), pursue a similar thought—"You are getting a huge amount of material and experience from a very, very simple starting point," as Eno says—and in a compositional context closer to *MFA*'s own.[31] Reich, who attended the initial rehearsals for *In C* and recommended that Riley give it a recurring pulse, reports that *It's Gonna Rain* was a way of a "working with repetition as a musical technique" in the context of composing music for voice as opposed to music for voice and text.[32] Based on recordings of a street preacher, Brother Walter, *It's Gonna Rain*, in two parts, involves constructed loops of Walter's voice that accentuate its "melody and meaning" while preserving its emotional power, as Reich puts it. This is particularly evident in Part 2, which revolves around scripture concerning the desperation of those trying to enter the ark after it had been sealed. (Listen from 0′42″ to 1′38″ and its repetition of phrases like "had been sealed," "couldn't open the door," and "cried, just open the door.") (▶ Audio 3.3) But that isn't what grabbed Eno, whose ambient work does not share the expressive goals of *It's Gonna Rain* and its gripping concretion of Cold War anxieties. What interests Eno is what took place when Reich ran his crafted loops in unison; they fell out of phase, which allowed repetition to generate novelty. "This process struck me," Reich writes, "as a way of going through a number of relationships between two identities without ever having any transitions. It was a seamless, uninterrupted process." And that gave Eno something of a template. As he recalled in 1996, "all of my ambient music, I should say, really was based on that kind of principle, on the idea that it's possible to think of a system or set of rules which once set in motion will create music for you."[33]

FIGURE 3.5 Steve Reich

Principles are not sounds, however, and relying on intuition and aesthetic judgment only goes so far. In fact, one needs to be careful with a term like "intuitive." It suggests a thoroughly unlearned, conceptless approach. But intuitions usually fire within a set of concrete possibilities, which exist, in turn, because of one's capabilities. Set a clarinet in my hands and I won't have many intuitions. I don't know enough to even play around. But I know how to use my voice, and so I will have intuitions if asked to sing, say, with regard to rhythm, volume, pitch, and the sonic character of various consonants and vowels. And my intuitions may also be led by certain conceptual positions: for example, that a voice should be just one part of the music (or its center), or that it should be natural (or heavily affected), expressive (or not), or, more broadly still, that a found sonic environment might be something to sing with rather than tuned out. Intuition thus needn't be opposed to training or conceptual thought. In fact, it often seems to build upon them. Nor should we take the affirmation of intuition to entail a thorough commitment to chance operations. In fact, those who take chance to be a defining force in their work, like Cage, often establish procedures to excise intuition from the generative process—"to remove themselves from the activities of the sounds they make"—as we saw in the radios of *Imaginary Landscape no. 4*.[34]

If we return to *MFA*, even in the absence of instrumental mastery, certain capacities are evident: working with and recording performers, electronically manipulating sounds, looping tapes, and mixing tones to establish a sonic field, to name four. How did Eno hone these skills? The answer is bound in part to a chance meeting. The musician Andy Mackay (b. 1946) had befriended Eno when the latter was at Winchester. Near the end of 1970, the two met on a train, and Mackay invited Eno to his band's practice in the hopes that Eno might record them. That was Eno's entrée into Roxy Music.

While several people came and went in Roxy Music's early days, the band that Eno accompanied featured the following cast, more or less. Bryan Ferry provided basic song structures and lyrics; he also sang and played keyboards. Andy Mackay played saxophone and oboe alongside Paul Thompson on drums and Graham Simpson on bass. After briefly serving as the band's roadie, Phil Manzanera took over guitar duties. The band had legitimate rock 'n' roll power. Thompson was rock steady and propelled the songs with unobtrusive but foot-tapping, even driving drum parts. Manzanera could solo with genuine fire, and Mackay had classical training. Listen to the first track on their self-titled debut album, "Re-make/Re-Model." It rocks. And it's clever. The ostensible subject appears to be a car termed "the sweetest queen I've ever seen"—the chorus sings a license plate number, CPL 593H. But the song is itself a remake or remodel of pop music itself, and the band goes a long ways toward making that plain. A lyric quotes "Femme Fatale" from the Velvet Underground, and during an instrumental break the bass quotes "Day Tripper" by the Beatles (3′26″–3′28″). Once we hear those gestures, the lyrics prove less certain, particularly the opening line, "I tried but I could not find a way." The actual subject may thus be pop music and its reassemblage, the car bit only a segment of a collage. This idea gains further traction when one remembers that the track opens with club or bar sounds, which suggests that every bit of the recording is a staging of something rather than an attempt at earnest expression. But none of these nuances diminish the power of the tune. "They were the conceptualists who could kick ass," Rob Chapman has written, and that about sums up the basic feel of Roxy Music's first two albums.[35]

One might suspect that Eno contributed the quoting, collage sensibility. But Ferry had studied with Richard Hamilton (1922–2011), who is often credited as a founder of pop art, thanks to the appearance of the word "Pop" (on a lollipop wrapper) in Hamilton's collage *Just what is it that makes today's homes, so appealing, so different?* (1956). Ferry was thus quite an image orchestrator. He even expected band members to dress glamorously, and he relied on collaboration from the fashion designer Anthony Price (b. 1945) to refine the non-musical aspects of their presentation. Down to hairstyles and shoes, then, the whole band was a collage of sorts, their name itself invoking a theater and, perhaps, their somewhat ironic approach to music—not quite rock but "Roxy," as David Shepherd suggests.[36]

What, then, did Eno contribute? The short answer is "treatments," though the first album, *Roxy Music*, specifies keyboards, synthesizer, tape, and tapes, which apparently entailed "two Revox reel-to-reel tape machines strung in sequence, the trusty Ferrograph tape recorder, an Ampex cassette recorder, a control keyboard, a customized delay unit and the all-important VCS3."[37] The last, whose full name is the Voltage Controlled Studio no. 3, is just that—a portable studio. It allowed the user to take inputs, manipulate them, and reintroduce (or patch) them into a signal that then went to tape or into the performance. And many manipulations were possible. The VCS3 included three oscillators, a shaper (or envelope generator, which grants control over things like attack and decay and allows one to introduce delays), and a noise generator, to name a few possibilities.[38]

The presumed "musicians" of Roxy Music thus provided Eno with a sonic palette that he could manipulate part by part as well as wash with an overall feel, or supplement, say with oscillating tones, as he does in "Re-make, Re-model" at 3′32″–3′37″, 3′50″–3′54," and 4′40″–4′50″. Speaking more generally, Peter Sinfeld, who produced the album, recalls that Eno "created an ambience and an environment and

FIGURE 3.6 Brian Eno of Roxy Music performing at Leicester University on November 18, 1972. Photo by Brian Cooke/Redferns.

he chopped up sounds with a VCS-3 synthesizer, doing similar tricks to what I'd done with Crimson."[39] You could also listen to the dissonant synthesizer wails on "Chance Meeting." (It could also be a treated guitar, though I don't think it matters much. In this song, the wail is the thing.) Entering around 0′35″, these reverberating and oscillating tones starkly contrast with a clean bass line, simple piano, and Ferry's plaintive voice. And the wail persists, even after Ferry reenters the song around 1′19″. In fact, it begins to overdetermine the mood, inflecting the evident longing of the song with something far less serene and gentle, particularly when Ferry again drops out and the piano goes into double time.

Eno's time with Roxy Music was relatively brief; he left in 1973. And whatever his reasons for leaving (lack of interest in live performance, power struggles with Ferry), his time in Roxy furthered his ability to work with sounds (and rework them) in a painterly fashion, adding textures, establishing layers, and introducing spaces, always with an ear for the overall feel of the track.[40] But even before he left, he had ventured into more experimental climes, collaborating with Robert Fripp (b. 1946), a founding member of King Crimson, whose music was at times much heavier than Roxy's, and far less ironic. As a guitarist, Fripp possesses strict and dazzling rhythmic capabilities, as well the ability to improvise in an emphatically lyrical, at times elegiac manner. And, like Eno, Fripp brought conceptual issues to the studio and stage.

In 1972 and '73, Eno and Fripp generated the music that became *(No Pussyfooting)*, which shows Eno the non-musician establishing a kind of compositional practice.[41] The album is built around interactions between Eno's tape-loop pieces and Fripp's work on electric guitar, which Eno would treat and feed back to Fripp. The results thus captured in a sonic stream the two responding to each other's responses, even though Eno is presumably still at work on "treatments." Across the album, Eno's atmosphere-setting efforts are no longer buried in songs but assert themselves as soundscapes. This is initially less apparent in the first track, "The Heavenly Music Corporation," because Fripp's soloing is so inspired and transporting. But his soaring licks don't commence until 2′30″. Prior to that, an expanding and contracting tone, like feedback, repeats and is joined by various other tones, including some pulses lasting three seconds and repeating after a second's rest, which gives the track something of a rhythmic feel, though not in any strict sense. Regardless, by the time Fripp begins soloing, something of an atmosphere has been established, and as a full contributor to the whole, as opposed to a treatment of the "properly musical" parts (▶ Audio 3.4). This feeling is intensified in the next track, the unhappily (and distractingly) titled "Swastika Girls," which begins with a coiling, insect-like sound that slowly (and modestly) builds across the opening minute and persists throughout.[42] When Fripp's guitar enters, its tone is compressed and the part limited to a simple, repeating chord, which also runs for the remainder of the piece. A third guitar part enters quietly just before the 3′00″ mark and is allowed to repeat, deep within the mix. A good deal of "Swastika Girls" is thus dense, Eno-scaped atmosphere. In both tracks, however, we find Eno the composer emerging, at least the Eno who offers music that aspires to the condition of painting. The music accrues by way of layers drawn from an electronic palette of tones. And the process whereby that is done is somewhat exposed, which intensifies its painterly feel—this composition was not conceived as a whole but built up. And because the mix establishes a wide stage of sound, the sense that one is hearing and even entering into a soundscape is quite palpable on even a modest stereo playback system.

Building upon the kind of work he could do in Roxy, and becoming increasingly at home in a world of electronic devices, *(No Pussyfooting)* allowed Eno to begin see the

FIGURE 3.7 Robert Fripp at Majestic Studios in 1973. Photo by John Davidson.

studio, even a portable one, as something like a musical instrument. Reflecting in 1995, he recalled:

> Processing, which is what that was, was at a very young stage: there was still this persistent idea that there was the musician who did his thing, then there was the producer who put on a bit of echo or something. The idea that there could be some real liaison between the person playing and the person doing the treatment was something quite new, and in fact, the first record I did with Fripp was exactly that: it was the two of us making one sound. . . . That kind of got me into the idea of the studio, not as a place for reproducing music but as a place for changing it, or re-creating it from scratch.[43]

Not that Eno inaugurated the idea that the studio could function like an instrument. In pop music, George Martin and the Beatles had used their studio's multitracking capacities to create songs like "Tomorrow Never Knows" from *Revolver* (1966). Assembled in part from various tracks that never belonged to a performance of the song, "Tomorrow Never Knows" was never played before it came together on tape. Such techniques then blossomed on *Pet Sounds* (1966) by the Beach Boys and achieved startling effect on *Sergeant Pepper's Lonely Hearts Club Band* (1967). Music was produced that had never been performed, as Eno himself observes.[44] But on *(No Pussyfooting)*, Eno fully embraced that approach to the studio to the point of leaving behind the very notion of a song, drawing heavily from the sonic turn. His tape loops establish the kind of inexact repetitions that mark his inheritance of some of La Monte Young's compositions, and his use of extended, non-pop durations (each track comes in at around twenty minutes) allows him to establish the kind of immersive soundscape achieved by Riley's *In C*, though without its insistent pulse.

Eno's studio capabilities continued to progress after his departure from Roxy. He began releasing albums under his own name, including *Another Green World* (1975), which remains a landmark in that it includes nine short instrumentals tracks without analog in the rock and pop music of the day. (The album's more typical songs are also among Eno's best.) As noted in the introduction, he worked with Bowie on *Low* and *Heroes*, and he produced albums for bands like Ultravox, Devo, and Talking Heads, as well as a compilation of underground music entitled *No New York* (1978). He also took note of what others were doing, like the dub-reggae producers King Tubby and Lee "Scratch" Perry, who often achieved novel sonic results by removing parts of a performance and manipulating the remainder in a manner that Eno likens to the work of a sculptor, much as Roger Maren did some twenty years earlier. "So much manipulation can be practiced on a recorded sound that it becomes almost as plastic as clay in the hands of a sculptor."[45]

In 1976 Eno spent significant time in Germany with the band Harmonia, composed of Michael Rother (of Neu!) and Hans-Joachim Roedelius and Dieter Moebius (of Cluster), participating in improvisational sessions at their commune/studio in Forst, West Germany. Further visits in 1977 found him recording two albums with Roedelius and Moebius, *Cluster & Eno* and *After the Heat*, the first in the studio of Conny Plank, a producer with sensibilities like

FIGURE 3.8 Eno in his home studio 1974. Photo by Erica Echenberg/Redferns

Eno's. "He was inspired," Eno recalls; "he thought that the job of being an engineer was highly creative."[46]

Because these various activities are documented in several good books, I won't cover them as steps toward *MFA*'s release in 1978, though no doubt they were.[47] Suffice it to say that each allowed Eno to turn the negations of the non-musician into something like a capability to work with sound in a manner that Eno calls "empirical." "You're working directly with sound, and there's no transmission loss between you and the sound—you handle it."[48] By 1979, Eno could say, "I don't really have a musical identity outside of studios."[49]

I have been taking the idea of the non-musician as a way of establishing oneself *within* musical practice. My account overlaps at points with Cecilia Sun's recent discussion of Eno's notion of the term, particularly regarding its abandonment of technical musical knowledge and instrumental virtuosity. However, she also observes something that adds an essential element to what I've said thus far. Namely, the absence of technical skills and knowledge may drive a certain kind of creativity. An inability to repeatedly execute the same function will introduce variety into a piece, and having definite limits may force one to seek variation in very simple procedures, which can be augmented by studio techniques. Becoming a non-musician, at least in Eno's case, thus involves learning to work with what knowledge and skill one does have, which may lead to some very interesting outcomes.[50]

One other set of associations is sufficiently integral to Eno's maturation that it bears recounting. During and after Roxy, Eno remained in conversation with the systems music scene in Britain. Thus, not only did Eno's time with the British avant-garde precede his participation and education in rock music, but he also seems to have remained in its currents for many of the years we have been reviewing. In fact, he used his prominence—and the financial backing it could garner—to sponsor a label, Obscure Records, to showcase avant-garde efforts and bring them to wider audiences.

Obscure Records released ten albums between 1975 and 1978. Featuring British composers such as Michael Nyman (b. 1944), David Toop (b. 1949), and Gavin Bryars, the series also presented work by American composers like Harold Budd (b. 1936), John Adams (b. 1947), and John Cage. This included Cage's piece for solo piano *In a Landscape* (1948), which seems to anticipate, in a very general way, the searching piano of *MFA*'s "1/2" and the sustained and contrasting single low note that resounds now and then in "1/1" (▶ Audio 3.5). While one might limit Eno's venture to the generous acknowledgment of and support for teachers and influences (Obscure no. 9 featured an opera written in part by Eno's former teacher Tom Philips), Eno was also sponsoring and in some cases producing music that captured, in part, a musical trend in line with his own developing sensibilities. In fact, he has justified the label in much the same way he justifies his ambient ventures. After recounting rock albums that depart from three- and four-minute songs in 4/4 time with traditional verse-chorus structures, he suggests, referring to his Obscure Records releases, "They all indicate that people are moving into a listening pattern that is far less dramatic and assaulting, they are capable of listening to pieces that go on for a time on a fairly level plateau and then fade

FIGURE 3.9 Gavin Bryars. Photo by Gautier Deblonde.

out and disappear. . . . Most of the Obscure Records have that characteristic—they exhibit a section from a continuum."[51]

Four of the ten albums released by Obscure Records feature work by Bryars, who also participated in the Scratch Orchestra, and whose spin-off venture, the Portsmouth Sinfonia, included Eno from 1970 to 1974.[52] These include the first in the series, *Jesus' Blood Never Failed Me Yet* (1975), which includes an eponymous piece as well as Bryars's *The Sinking of the Titanic*. This suggests, I think, that Bryars was particularly central to Eno's continued presence and work in the British avant-garde. A brief look at the first album shows why. Both pieces have much in common with the kind of work that Eno had commenced with Fripp on *(No Pussyfooting)*. They are extended, avoid complex developments or musical structures, accrue variety by layering sounds over repetitions, have a common progenitor (Steve

FIGURE 3.10 The Portsmouth Sinfonia at the Queen Elizabeth Hall in 1972. Courtesy of The Portsmouth Sinfonia and Peter Fowler.

FIGURE 3.11 Brian Eno and Sinfonia conductor John Farley in Majestic Studios, London, September 1973. Photo by Doug Smith. Courtesy of the Portsmouth Sinfonia and Doug Smith.

Reich), and seem to welcome a variety of attentions, from immersion to hearing as background music. In fact, two reviewers describe Bryars's work on Obscure no. 1 as a kind of easy listening, and Eno echoed the thought in an interview with Keith Ansell, even as he applied it to his own contribution to the label.[53]

Eno's *Discreet Music* (1975), which he views as similar in function to *The Sinking of the Titanic*, was the third record released on Obscure Records.[54] It is a clear predecessor to *MFA*. At least in the case of the title track, it fully liberated the kind of soundscape that kept receding behind Fripp's guitar on *(No Pussyfooting)*. It also concretized what has become something of a signature of Eno's ambient work, the fade-in and fade-out, which suggests that the music on hand is "a section from a continuum." Other studio techniques were integral to its composition as well: echo, delay, looping of sound material, avoiding discernible rhythms, and the manipulation of playback speed as a way of controlling pitch and duration (▶ Audio 3.6). *Discreet Music* thus evidences the full transformation of the non-musician into the studio impresario. Eno still eschews technical knowledge and virtuosity, and he remains willing to trust in aesthetic judgment, but he is now able to generate a free-standing musical piece that holds its own within a collection of works operating within the sonic turn.[55]

But something else also came to fruition with "Discreet Music," and it is tied less to compositional procedures than to the piece's social function. As noted, Eno was attracted to the easy-listening character of works like Bryars's. But he also imagined that this kind of accessibility, already operative in Riley's *In C*, could prove even more interesting when rendered without significant dynamics, development, or musical complexity and allowed to unfold over a sufficiently long period of time—*Discreet Music* runs for over half an hour. "It's intended as music you don't have to concentrate on," he told Adrian Jack. He continued:

> It's like adding to your ambience, changing the condition of the room a little bit. If you want to focus on another level, there's a set of ideas that are interesting in terms of systems working like Steve Reich's *It's Gonna Rain.* And to stop it from being monotonous—and, I suppose, completely ignorable—I did make changes during the piece. This touching up is very much a philistine idea in experimental composers' terms; it's wanting to entertain. But I think the borderline area is a very interesting one.[56]

At this point, Eno was poised to make *MFA*, whose liner notes claim that the album "must be as ignorable as it is interesting." In fact, *Discreet Music* is undoubtedly Eno's first ambient work, which is why Eno cites Satie in its liner notes. It is thus time for us to explore what "ambient" entails, what kind of ambience *MFA* initiates, and how (and to what degree) the album is *for* airports.

CHAPTER 4
AMBIENCE

The problem is that people don't realize that music actually does things to them, not just entertain.

—Eno, in "Math Qualities of Music Interest Eno"

Before *MFA* even appeared, Eno was recounting what motivated him to produce work like *Discreet Music*. Judy Nylon (b. 1948), then a punk rocker, visited Eno as he recovered from an accident—he had been run over by a taxi. She brought him harp music. After she left, he played the album at low volume. Only one speaker worked consistently, however, and it was raining outside. The music sort of came and went and mixed with the rainfall. It also blended unevenly with Eno's wavering, painkiller awareness. "And I began to think of environmental music—music deliberately constructed to occupy the background. And I realized that muzak was a very strong concept."[1] Nylon remembers things differently. They more or less intentionally set the music to play with the rain: "There was no 'ambience by mistake.' Neither of us invented ambient music."[2]

Irrespective of its veracity, Eno's story tells us something important about ambient music: it is not indifferent to the world in which it appears. It situates itself, explicitly and interactively, along a distinctly porous border that distinguishes music from the world in which it resounds—say, a performance onstage from a concert hall, or a stereo from people chatting in a living room, or wherever you and your headphones go from the sound emanating from your earbuds. Ambient music is designed to negotiate and to a certain degree expose what conjoins these phenomena.

As the liner notes to *Discreet Music* observe, music that explicitly addresses and engages its social-sonic environment—listeners included—has strong ties to Erik Satie, who also identified as a non-musician.[3] In 1920, Satie ventured *musique d'ameublement*—furniture music. Composed to accompany an intermission for a play by Max Jacob (1876–1944) and scored with help from Darius Milhaud, the piece was performed on instruments distributed around the theater. A program note instructed the audience to give the performers no more attention than they would give the "candelabra, the seats, or the balcony."[4] The play's organizer, Pierre Bertin, explained that the music "claims to make a contribution to life in the same way as a private conversation, a painting in a gallery, or the chair on which you may or may not be seated. You will be trying it out."[5] Apparently, the audience rebelled. They listened attentively. The first enactment of furniture music thus failed. It either wasn't

FIGURE 4.1 A postage stamp commemorating Erik Satie

innocuous enough or the audience was not up to the task of giving it less than their full attention. But in their defense, the instructions were ambiguous—one doesn't look at a painting like one sits in a chair, and a private conversation seems different still.

Satie's notebook jottings are clearer.[6] They term furniture music "industrial," "designed to satisfy *utility* requirements," thereby contrasting it with music that seeks to be art. "Art does not come into these requirements." Nor is the music expressive: "*Furniture Music* has no first name," meaning it does not express the thoughts and/or feelings of a particular person. It is rather *for* some situation. What it has is a setting, and Satie imagined several possible locales: an assembly hall, a lobby, a shop window. In fact, he was insistent that many settings need furniture music. "No meetings, assemblies etc. without furniture music." Furniture music is thus more like a chair than a painting in a gallery. One sits in rather than contemplates the chair. So too furniture music: it "creates vibration; it has no other purpose; it fills the same role as light, warmth and comfort in all its forms."

As Satie notes, his is not the first music to limit itself to accompaniment; some waltzes, fantasias, marches, and polkas had similar aims. And we can add other phenomena to his list, such as music designed to accompany grand meals, so-called table music, whose roots lie in the sixteenth century. And so too divertimenti, which came to prominence in the eighteenth century and were designed to "serve as background music for some social gathering such as a conversation or a banquet."[7] But Satie's effort does distinguish itself, both in its efforts to accompany more than aristocratic gatherings and in its specificity—assembly halls, lobbies, and shop windows.

Furniture music's proximity to ambient music is clear. Speaking with Anthony Korner about *MFA*, Eno said, "The underlying idea was to try to suggest that there were new places to put music, new kinds of niches where music could belong."[8] Moreover, Eno's ambience is akin to Satie's light and warmth:

> An ambience is defined as an atmosphere, or a surrounding influence: a tint. My intention is to produce original pieces ostensibly (but not exclusively) for particular times and situations with a view to building up a small but versatile catalogue

of environmental music suited to a wide variety of moods and atmospheres.[9]

Note, though, that Eno imagines a more flexible catalogue of works. Moreover, he does not limit ambient music to the background; that is just one of its possible functions. "Ambient Music must be able to accommodate many levels of listening attention without enforcing one in particular." Bertin's diverse analogies seem more apropos to Eno's efforts, therefore, than to Satie's. Finally, in imagining its impress—what it does to us—Eno conceives of something a bit more specific than light: a tint, hence Eno's emphasis on mood. Eno associates *MFA* with a sense of calm, which I take to be more than the simple absence of anxiety; it connotes a readiness, even serenity. "2/2," with its faux horns swelling and receding, has the effect of lapping water. One can wade in its comings and goings, buoyed by its continuity (no rests, no silences, no key changes), as well as its subtle variations and micro-dynamics, which give the track a slight but supple energy. The effect is soothing, but the variations also prompt a kind of alertness, even as they do not call attention to themselves, at least not principally. Henry Jenkins seems to register this kind of impact when he writes: "I often use Eno's music as a backdrop when I am writing and I like to listen to this strangely familiar (and I do mean strange) music when I have trouble relaxing in strangely familiar hotel rooms while traveling."[10]

Cage looms between Satie and Eno, and Eno probably read Cage's 1958 essay "Erik Satie" in *Silence*. It is difficult to imagine Eno not taking note of a claim like this one: "It is evidently a question of bringing one's intended actions into relation with the ambient unintended ones."[11] And yet Eno's ambient work is closer to Satie's than to Cage's appropriation, which tries to absorb Satie into a total commitment to the activity of sounds. "To be interested in Satie," Cage wrote, "one must be disinterested to begin with, accept that a sound is a sound and a man is a man, give up illusions about ideas of order, expressions of sentiment, and all the rest of our inherited claptrap."[12] Keeping to musical furniture, Cage's imperative is partly true. Expression is beside the point. But this does not evidence complete disinterest. In fact, Satie is quite insistent, if playfully so, that various settings are in need of musical emendation. "Do not enter a house which does not use furniture music," he urged.[13] So yes, it is a question of "bringing one's intended actions into relation with the ambient unintended ones," but whereas Cage would erase the differences between them, Eno, like Satie, aims to enrich the latter with the former.

Eno's distance from Cage and nearness to Satie (at least regarding musical furniture) opens a continuum along which one can set various ambient efforts.[14] At one extreme lies Cage's *4′33″*. It effaces itself to underscore the activity of whatever sounds accompany the performance. Next, one could imagine music that hovers in the background and remains there, and so stands in the line of table music, divertimenti, and musical furniture, which Satie hoped might complement café culture, neutralizing street noises, filling awkward silences, and "softening the clatter of knives and forks without dominating them."[15] Beside such purely background efforts we then could set music that works its way into the situation, tuning it, as *MFA* purports to do, and with varying degrees of intensity—recall that Jenkins listens to Eno in order to relax in hotel rooms as well as to write.

Some ambient music, including some of Eno's, is more immersive than *MFA*. "And immersion was really the point," he has said, thinking of the ambient series as a whole; "we were making music to swim in, to float in, to get lost inside."[16] It is difficult for me to think of "1/1" in this register, even though "2/2" approximates such an effect. Yes, "1/1" beguiles, but it also eludes. With nothing to follow, and with ongoing variations, immersion is interrupted. Eno's *Ambient 4: On Land* (1982) is better suited for those seeking immersion. Even less musical than *MFA*, at least in a traditional sense (one rarely if ever hears instruments), and even more painterly, the album is nevertheless almost programmatic in being related to a sense of place, albeit an imaginary place.

> What qualified a piece for inclusion on the record was that it took me somewhere, but this might be somewhere that I'd never been before, or somewhere I'd only imagined going to. Lantern Marsh, for example, is a place only a few miles from where I grew up in East Anglia, but my experience of it derives not from having visited it (although I almost certainly did) but from having subsequently seen it on a map and imagining where and what it might be. We feel affinities not only with the past, but also with the futures that didn't materialize, and with the other variations of the present that we suspect run parallel to the one we have agreed to live in.[17]

If you listen to the initial thirty-five seconds of "Lantern Marsh," you'll hear an expanding and contracting set of tones (hovering between C and C♯), various bird and (presumably) reptile sounds, others that sound like short bursts of wind, and a deep, resonating bass tone that lasts for several seconds (which recurs at various points across the piece) (▶ Audio 4.1). Right away, therefore, one finds oneself is something like a marsh. Then around 1′08″ one begins to increasingly hear warbling at a higher register than the introductory tones until, around 1′55″ or so, it is difficult not to hear what could be voices carried by the wind. While somewhat haunting, they also carry a kind of cheer, which gives the track a general feeling of serenity, as if one had chanced upon a circuit of operations—here an ecosystem—maintaining itself without stress or worry.

As you may have noticed, the continuum I have in mind for ambient music involves relative increases in the degree of atmosphere or tint brought to the hearing or listening situation. And one could imagine (and find) even more immersive music. The "deep listening" pursued and facilitated by Pauline Oliveros (1932–2016) and her associates Stuart Dempster (b. 1936) and David Gamper (1945–2011) derives from this kind of deeply immersive music, which also has roots in the work of La Monte Young. Like Satie's furniture music, vibrations lie at its core, but they are intended to absorb the world in which and with which they resound. "Deep Listening is a form of meditation," writes Oliveros. "Attention is directed to the interplay of the sounds and silences or the sound/silence continuum. . . . The relationship of all perceptible sounds is important."[18] "Lear," from the album *Deep Listening* (1989), gives one a feel for this. But given its emphasis on actual interactions, I won't gloss a reading or a listening. Instead, listen to it at a reasonably loud volume and allow it to envelop you. Not that you need

FIGURE 4.2 Pauline Oliveros. Photo by Pieter Kers.

to be still or sitting; but listen "deeply"—attend to all resonant environments and their interactions.

On my view, then, "ambient" names a variable function that music can play—it engages its environment in ways that establish atmospheres and tints, even moods. I say this in part because the processes and technologies determining its construction can prove wildly variable. Sounds generated through tape loops can function in an ambient manner, but so can music written, performed, and recorded in the most traditional manner. Analogously, one can play most recordings of traditionally composed and performed classical or even rock music in an ambient fashion simply by lowering the volume. And one can focus on the activity of sounds in almost any recording. While music intended to function in an ambient manner probably should avoid profound dynamics and acute dissonance, the musical features of a given piece depend on the environment and the desired mood. A loud club or party may want a consistent and palpable beat, and the noise of the scene may absorb many tones and changes that would seem strident in more intimate settings.

I thus think it is useful to understand the "ambient" venture as one that concerns how music interacts with larger acoustic and social settings. It is not designed to fully absorb the attention of those who hear it, but to interact with them nevertheless, resulting in a determinate atmosphere that tints the music, the listener, and those points at which they meet. At its extremes, however, this character begins to blur. *4′33″* offers too little and deep listening too much by way of atmosphere to be paradigmatic instances of ambient music. But each still aims to engage its surroundings and thereby to change one's orientation to those surroundings. A continuum at and between ambient music's extremes does persist, therefore, when, in Satie's words, people "make music on occasions with which music has *nothing* to do," at least typically.[19]

If "ambient" names a function more than any clear set of musical traits, it becomes easier to understand why the genre includes so much diversity, including subgenres: ambient house, dark ambient, ambient industrial, illbient, ambient dub, ambient classical, and so on. (Even the fourth album in Eno's own series, *On Land*, is appreciably different than *MFA*, as we have seen.) Moreover, thinking of "ambient" in a functional matter discourages us from treating *MFA* as an urtext for most of the ambient efforts that have appeared in its wake. But this may be as Eno would have it. If "music" names a cybernetic system (or set of systems), then *MFA* is an event that has led to variety (in Eno's sense), not identity or even obvious continuity. One finds beat-oriented ambient works such as Moby's *Ambient* (1993) and Aphex Twin's *Selected Ambient Works: 1985–1992*. Aphex Twin's "Actium" repeats (more or less) a bass figure for roughly seven and a half minutes, though it drops out at two points and is later subjected to modest adjustments. Various electronic sounds are layered atop the bass figure, often rhythmically deployed, and simple, improvisational electric piano parts, offset, every now and then, with contrasting rhythms (▶ Audio 4.2). "My Beautiful Sky," by Moby, in 4/4 time, layers a simple, repeating synthesizer melody atop consistent pulse beats, with an occasional break, such as the introduction of a short piano phrase between 1′40″ and 1′48″, or a more extended rhythmic interlude from 2′40″ to 3′20″ followed by a return to the basic synthesizer melody. It sounds more like a dance tune designed to let those on the floor catch their breath than an imagined landscape such as "Lantern Marsh" or a thought-prompting inducement like *MFA*'s "1/2."

Many ambient works abandon any obvious center of attention, offering even less sonic material than *MFA*. Thomas Köner's "Permafrost," from his 1993 album of the same name, consists of little more than lower-register, rumbling sounds subjected to massive reverb and echo, resulting in a sound that calls to mind wind traveling across an empty, barren—and presumably frozen—landscape. (Nothing like the sustained ecology of "Lantern Marsh" can be found.) (▶ Audio 4.3) Wolfgang Vogt, who releases music under his own name as well as the moniker Gas, produces beat-driven pieces but also soundscapes that seem uninhabited or at best haunted. His "Zauberberg V" (1997) is built around a recurring beat: one-two, one-two, one-two, one-two. Distant ambient noises, industrial in character, line the soundstage at an audible distance. The space evoked is huge and inhuman; its effect is far from calm (▶ Audio 4.4). Despite the space, one feels claustrophobic as the track progresses. When the beat subsides around the seven-minute mark, waves of industrial sound continue, with the occasional synthesizer chord resounding with indifference.[20]

Something closer to dreamlike vistas opens in the work of the ambient composer Robert Scott Thompson, as with "Submerged" from his album *Frontier* (1998), though the track also stays true to its name and begins to play with deep, reverbing rumbles at 2′20″. The result contrasts different ambient spaces and brings a sense of narrative development to the piece, as if the listener is traversing locales, much as one does in extended dreams. (▶ Audio 4.5 contains a passage from "Submerged"). In this case, then, ambient music seems open to narrative, whereas *MFA* conspicuously avoids it, particularly on tracks "1/2" and "2/2."

Recently, Max Richter composed *Sleep* (2015), an eight-hour piece combining synthesizers, organ, piano, voice, and strings that is designed to work its way into whatever kind of awareness persists while sleeping. It less imagines dream spaces than seeks to enter and influence them. "We spend more time sleeping than we do anything else," he writes in his liner notes. "What a miraculous part of our lives. . . . What happens to music here? Are there ways in which music and consciousness can interact other than in a wakeful state?"[21] Like *MFA*, *Sleep* seems to explore regions of life usually neglected by traditional music. But here the goal seems closer to Ambien than ambience.

One could keep extending this list of composers and artists whose work intersects with the term "ambient" in one way or another, including William Basinski, as well as groups like Labradford and Stars of the Lid. And that doesn't even scratch the surface. Since 2001, Wolfgang Vogt has curated a Pop Ambient series, indicating that the genre is only growing vaster and more diffuse. Looking at the genre from the inception of *MFA*, it is apparent that only some works employ clear melodies. Some are rhythmic, some not. Most are quiet with limited dynamics, but not all. Acoustic instruments are integral to some ambient works while others are wholly electronic. Some make use of silence. Others saturate the listening field. Some go nowhere, as Eno says, while others admit of a kind of development. "Ambient" is thus a loose genre. But in every case, or almost every case—there are always exceptions—something like an intervention in an extra-musical scene takes place. Ambient works are thus almost always *for* something other than their own performance or enactment: chill rooms, parties, bars and clubs, meditation, or a general backdrop secured through earbuds, even sleep. They reach out toward the lives they wash over. What Garry Cobain says of the efforts of his group FSOL, an experimental, house-ambient duo, applies more broadly to the genre. "What our music . . . represents is a weird perspective on this space now. It's like a re-evaluation of yourself in your space."[22]

Eno once told Paul Merton: "Very much the message of ambient music for me was that this is music that be located in life, not in opposition to life."[23] Similar efforts can be found in multiple twentieth-century figures and movements. The philosopher John Dewey's *Art as Experience* (1938) argues for more attention to the aesthetic potentials of everyday life, and the various composers and artists associated with FLUXUS (including La Monte Young, at least initially) generated numerous performance pieces that alerted their audiences to the ways in which everyday activities might contain artistic dimensions.[24] Consider *Drip Music* (1959) by George Brecht (1926–2008), which Eno performed twice at Winchester. Existing in three versions, it asks a performer to drip a liquid, in one case into "an empty vessel . . . so that the water falls into the vessel" and in another case, very slowly, into the "bell of a French horn or tuba held in the playing position by a second performer at floor level." (The third just says: "Dripping." Your faucet may perform it several times a day.)[25] The logic animating such performances is clear: if you demystify art, an enlivened everyday awaits.

Outside the avant-garde, other forces were also working to integrate music into daily life. Brigadier General George Owen Squier (1865–1934), a career radio engineer, founded Wired Radio in 1922, hoping to send musical signals into homes and businesses. (He changed the name of his company to Muzak in 1934, shortly before his death.[26]) As it evolved and other businesses became its chief subscribers, Muzak ceased transmitting previously recorded material. To control their musical contours and better integrate them into subscriber locales, it began producing and recording its own versions of familiar pieces. And formats were established for particular kinds of businesses. In scenes devoted principally to production, the goal was clear: "to supply its clients with a program of tunes segmented by mood as a tonic for the times of day when the human spirit sags."[27] But restaurants and diners could also subscribe, so Muzak also sought to stimulate consumption, perhaps by coloring the brand of available goods and services.

With the emergence of the LP in 1948, it became easier to introduce mood music into middle-class homes. In the 1950s, Capitol Records had a "Background Music" line, and RCA, under the direction of orchestrator George Melachrino, released a "Moods in Music" series that "supplied an audiologue of varying tempers and situations: studying, romancing, dining, working, courage and inspiration, or just daydreaming."[28] The music was often cinematic, hinting at a narrative backdrop for one's comings and goings. It provided less the soundtrack to your life than a soundtrack for a life one might hope to live. Consider "Dusk," the lead track on *Music for Daydreaming* (1954). A slow waltz performed with little to no energy, scored for lush strings and an occasional pizzicato complement, "Dusk" sounds like a soundtrack for an interlude in a love story—parted lovers long for one another and seek solace in recollections. And one sees an image of just that on the album cover, which provides a top-down view of a woman reclining in an armchair, her chest partially exposed, her look wistful, even melancholy. She could be you or thinking of you, the music suggests.

Like all the lineages I have traced, this recounting of ambient music is truncated. Phenomena other than the avant-garde, Muzak, and mood music pertain to the emergence of *MFA*. One other source demands at least passing notice, as Eno himself notes. With the availability of film scores on LP, one could repurpose soundtracks as background music for one's own life. In the absence of the films, the "listener . . . became the population of a sonic landscape and was free to wander 'round it."[29] While Eno recalls Nino Rota's work on Fellini's films, Popol Vuh's evocative scores for Werner Herzog's work also come to mind as correlates to ambient music from the sixties and seventies (▶ Audio 4.6). Play the soundtrack without the film and one has an atmosphere for one's own affairs. No wonder one finds some proto-ambient pieces, albeit short ones, on Eno's 1976 collection *Music for Films*, which includes many tracks he assembled without any particular film in mind (▶ Audio 4.7). It is unsurprising, therefore, that many regard ambient music as soundtracks for their lives.

While Muzak and mood music are overtly ingratiating, they remain analogous to ambient music regarding its intended function: to dynamically enjoin music with situations in which they are heard. When asked about mood music, British producer Norrie Paramor (1914–79) said: "It's very difficult to define. . . . I imagine it's meant to entertain without being obtrusive, to put you in an easy frame of mind. In other words, perhaps it is music to be heard, but not necessarily listened to."[30] The proximity is evident. Not only does "entertain without being obtrusive" somewhat approximate Eno's insistence that ambient music be interesting and ignorable while not enforcing itself, but Paramor is also paraphrasing Milhaud's characterization of furniture music—to be heard, not listened to.

Yet Eno also distinguishes *MFA* (and ambient music more generally) from Muzak, which Eno was already rethinking in 1972. "Right now, I'm very interested in Muzak as a form," he told Nick Kent. "I used to suffer from long stretches of insomnia and was forced to construct a piece using tape-loops that took the form of Muzak which, in turn, was conducive to sleep. Really, the potential to be found in the use of electronic music has only just begun to be mined."[31] More generally, it also seems that Muzak underwhelmed *Roxy Music.* In 1973, Bryan Ferry bemoaned the tedium of travel. "Sitting in a Muzak-bombarded lounge tends to turn you into a vegetable more than it inspires you—unless you see something amazing, or someone walks past with a poodle or something. But those are quite rare."[32]

How does Muzak fall short? The background it provides stimulates listeners in various ways—bringing energy when it lags, or layering a shopping mall with the sounds of contentment: predictable harmonies, a recurring motif or chorus, and rhythms that are easy to track, never frantic, and thus agreeable. As the insert for *MFA* indicates, however, "Ambient Music is intended to induce calm and a space to think." Without appreciable rhythms, and in the absence of pronounced dynamic changes, each track calms by being calm. Like much of the time it fills, it proceeds without distinct beginnings, middles, and endings, and thus does not build anticipation. Nor in the absence of developing motifs does it gather and fasten one's attention. And because there is no clearly defined tonic key from which to stray or return, the music does not build a desire or need for resolution. Broadly, then, *MFA* moves "away from narrative and towards landscape," as Eno says of ambient music generally.[33] And as it does so, *MFA* also exploits timbres that, while never harsh, are odd and modestly surprising. Moreover, the absence of rhythm is somewhat disorienting. Unable to settle into recurring patterns, one is unable to predict what will arrive. *MFA* doesn't remove uncertainty and doubt, therefore. Instead, it introduces a kind of uncertainty amid calm, and this is what opens something like a space to think, one that remains open-ended, given Eno's avoidance of familiar material. In fact, *MFA*'s somewhat amorphous and discontinuous sonic material seems to suspend its listeners somewhere in the space between hearing and listening.

Among *MFA*'s four tracks, "1/2" provides the strongest example of such an intervention. Keeping to its opening, one hears two distinct piano parts played atop one another, but without any discernable rhythmic alignment. Certain tones thus jar in a modest way, such as the conjunction at 0′13″. (Listen also to the piano overlays from 1′02″ through 1′19″.) (▶ Audio 4.8). The searching quality of each piano, however, as well as an occasional long sustain, keeps the procession gentle, a feeling thickened by the arrival and departure of ethereal vocal tones (more "ahhhhhs"). Not that the track necessarily effects reflection, but it does not pad our awareness with familiarity or a consistent rhythm, and so it does seem qualitatively distinct from Muzak.

After an experience in 1977, Eno began assembling *MFA*'s calming, reflective tracks for use in airports. Awaiting a flight in Cologne, Eno wondered "what kind of music would sound good in a building like that," particularly among people about to fly, who were thus somewhat "apprehensive."[34] One thing that didn't work, Eno thought, was Muzak. It seemed to irritate rather than comfort. Why? Presumably by trying to erase every flyer's reasonable apprehension—planes crash, and even experienced fliers chuckle uneasily in turbulence. Eno's alternative was music that could induce serenity while working with airport sounds, such as announcements, which meant it needed to be somewhat unobtrusive and withstand interruptions. Given the absence of motifs subject to development, there isn't any readily apprehensible, unfolding process to interrupt among *MFA*'s four tracks, and its placid dynamics render it unassuming. Its form thus suits its function in a general way. And on occasion, *MFA* has indeed been played in airports. Shepherd reports installations in New York, Minneapolis-Saint Paul, and São Paolo–Guarulhos, and Bang on a Can have offered live performances of their scored versions at the UK airport Stansted (1998) and in Düsseldorf (2011).[35]

And yet it seems overly narrow, even misleading, to think of *MFA* as principally *for* airports. First, Eno introduced the ambient series as a "small catalogue of environmental music suited to a *wide variety* of moods and atmospheres."[36] The album is thus designed to accommodate multiple settings. But more importantly, *MFA* is an album, an LP. Because it was not composed with musical notation but generated with various runs of tape, its length and sonic character reflect its principal way of sounding forth—the phonograph or, to a lesser extent, a cassette deck, and in either case a stereo system of some sort. (If one tethers music to resonant environments, to recall Lucier, *MFA* is "music for stereo reproduction" in the way that more traditional music might be "music for string trio in a chamber.") But in 1978, airports were unlikely to project LPs or cassettes throughout terminals. As Eno observed in 1986: "When you make a record you are making it for a living room."[37] What *MFA* induces, therefore—what it is for—concerns a broader range of life than what comes and goes in airports.

To appreciate the broader impact that *MFA* might offer, we need to consider some of Eno's other theoretical commitments. Alongside cybernetics, Eno is a student of Morse Peckham (1914–93), who theorized art's evolutionary role through a theory of drives. Peckham held that phenomena such as selective emphasis in visual perception indicate a drive for order that, because it trades in generalities, ignores large swaths of experience and risks monotony—"The drive to order is also a drive to get stuck in the mud."[38] Art, he argued, indicates that something else also operates. "There must, it seems to me, be some human activity which serves to break up orientations, to weaken and frustrate the tyrannous drive to order, to prepare the individual to observe what the orientation tells him is irrelevant, but what very well may be highly relevant."[39] Art creates a space—a physically safe space, Peckham thinks—in which ephemeral facets of the world can appear, say, the activity of sounds, and with enough intensity that we find ourselves between our normal orientations and a newly emerging one, such as an appreciation for the aesthetic dimension of the everyday.

But even art gets stuck, say, in the major scale and its harmonic orders. How, then, does one rejuvenate one's efforts? In writing about *Another Green World*, Geeta Dayal pays a great deal of attention to *Oblique Strategies*, a stack of cards designed by Eno and the painter Peter Schmidt (1931–80).[40]

To be picked at random, each card carries a phrase designed to reorient creative activity. Here are three: "Look at the order in which you do things"; "Slow preparation . . . fast execution"; "Allow an easement. (An easement is the abandonment of a stricture.)" Such cards, as well as the use of such cards, tells us a great deal about Eno's understanding of creativity: it eludes the inertia of one's usual way of doing things. Not that one can do without any ordered way of doing things. Taking his bearings from cybernetics, Eno works through interventions rather than utterly spontaneous creations. The variety he finds through systems music came from the system, after all. And therein lies the key—one takes steps to outwit oneself, whether with an oblique strategy or a pattern (or system) with which to generate sounds. That is, one initiates activities that run counter to one's habits, and one awaits the results, judgment at the ready. (Recall that judgment is one of the cardinal qualities that Eno affirms when he negates the idea of "the musician" as an agent of technique and mastery. "I'm proud enough to trust my own judgment," Eno told David Sterrit. "And when it's time to follow a new thread, it always seems like fresh territory."[41])

To my mind, *MFA* functions a bit like an oblique strategy, and along Peckham's lines. It arrives as an easement into one's current activities and awareness, loosening the logic of both and replacing them with an indeterminate mood, like calm. Recall this claim: "Ambient Music must be able to accommodate many levels of listening attention without enforcing one in particular; it must be as ignorable as it is interesting." My point rephrases this a bit. *MFA* is too interesting to be ignored and too diffuse to be followed.

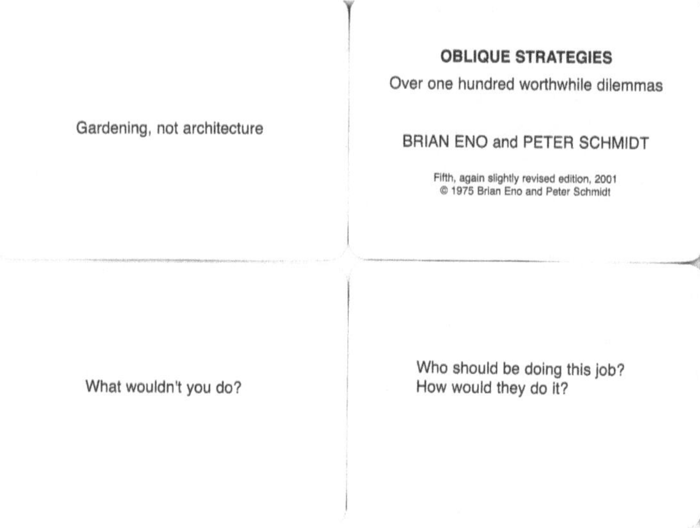

FIGURE 4.3 Three oblique strategies

There just isn't enough compositional structure to force our attention. And if we submit to what is on offer, the asynchronous activity of various assemblages of sounds, we submit to a kind of easement in a scene of relative safety. Our attention is drawn away from the habits and orders of the day, and we find ourselves in the wake of that suspension, but amid calming musical successions.

Is there a name for this result? Reverie, I think, from *resver, rever*, "to wander," "to be delirious," with connotations of daydreaming. I don't mean this in any technical sense, such as Wilfred Bion's psychoanalytic usage, which names a mother's loving openness that supports the fluctuating condition and demands of the infant, or Gaston Bachelard's association of reverie with the generation of images in poetic and mythic consciousness, though both carry relevant connotations. Rather, I have in mind a kind of pleasant perplexity—what is this, where is it going, how am I to respond? As David Toop says of ambient music more generally, it encourages "states of reverie and receptivity in the listener that suggest (on the good side of boredom) a very positive rootlessness."[42]

The emergence of a dislocated preparedness is something Eno associates with art in general, again following Peckham. "The biological function of art is that it should expose you to disorientation. When you are confronted by an artist, he should present you with a situation which violates the expectations which he arouses."[43] But we shouldn't exaggerate the negativity of the work's impact. Searching piano phrases, surprising juxtapositions and overlays as well as timbral shimmers within a calm succession of sounds induces alertness as well, even curiosity. I would thus insist on taking reverie, at least in this context, as a multidimensional awareness distinguished by (a) its felt departure from an initial disposition or expectation, (b) its relatively calm mood, (c) its lack of a prescribed object, and (d) its readiness for whatever comes its way, which may involve the sounds of *MFA*, the quality of one's own listening, the resonance of one's environment, the feeling of one's posture, or the imagined variables of an impending journey.

The kind of reverie that I associate with *MFA* is distinct from the "deep listening" we discussed earlier. Deep listening cosmically integrates the listener into a field of vibrations. It pursues a meditative state. "Music can be a model for universal structure," La Monte Young has suggested, "because we perceive sound as vibration and if you believe, as I do, that vibration is the key to universal structure you can understand why I make this statement."[44] *MFA* operates at a more mundane level. It takes the world as it is—bedroom, airport, a city walk, or doing the dishes—and nudges us toward a fresh encounter with something far more particular than universal structures: water on the plate, serenity before a flight, a new place to plant one's tulips, a slightly different way to hear the "ahhhhhs" on "1/2."

It is important to underscore that the path of reverie is a two-way street. If you are too tired, the album may put you to sleep. If you are performing an activity that requires significant attention like driving, one's reverie will be foreshortened. (New uses for one's car may be unwelcome.) If one is over caffeinated, the music will lag, perhaps even irritate. To take the world as it is, *MFA* needs to engage the world as it is, and that marks a dependency. This is not the kind of art that establishes and institutes the conditions of its own reception—that would require it to enforce one kind of attention, namely, the kind of absorption valorized by art historian Michael Fried, which I associate with the works of high modernism.[45] The internal relations of their elements, including their form and/or genre, exemplify a singular logic that one must labor to decipher. One could say they establish an art world and insistently remain there, situating audiences as critics and connoisseurs. *MFA* enters life differently—obliquely, gently, but nevertheless, at least on occasion, transformatively.

MFA might impact subjectivity in other ways as well. Anahid Kassabian has initiated a study of what she terms "ubiquitous musics" that accompany activities (driving, shopping, eating in a restaurant) and events (commercials, parties, political rallies). On her view, when music backgrounds these phenomena, it helps them stage various identities. For example, jazz helps brand a coffee shop and establish a scene for those that frequent it (as would punk music). Or 1980s pop music in a grocery store tells a certain demographic (my own, at least generationally and ethnically): "You belong here." Much like sacred music, which reinforces identities operative in rituals, ubiquitous music can intensify a sense of who we are, particularly as it stirs the affects. One finds oneself fallen but open to redemption, chosen or beloved by a god. And identities need this kind of recognition on her view. Identity "doesn't reside within a single subject; rather, it is a flow across a field, which constantly morphs into different shapes and contours, depending on the circumstances."[46] Ubiquitous music is thus integral to what Kassabian terms "distributed subjectivity," a sense of self varied and flowing from different social locations.

I share Kassabian's position in a general way, although a constantly morphing sense of self cries out for a concept other than "identity." Still, like "God Bless America" at a baseball game, music can mark and thus reinforce (or exclude) a certain *sense of self* (which would be my preferred term).[47] But for ubiquitous music to intensify "identities," it needs to have some clear, cultural currency or ethnic-historical location. Not just any song will intensify a sense of belonging to a god-graced militarized empire during a baseball game, and not just any song or set of songs will tell me "you belong" when I shop for dinner.

While a leading example of ambient music, *MFA* is not a broadly known or popular album. Should it be played in a public space, therefore, few would recognize it quickly, and only a few more would recognize it at all. I thus wonder how and to what degree it stages identities in contexts of ubiquitous listening. Let's return to a coffee shop with people reading, writing, or chatting. The coming and going of *MFA* or *On Land* could certainly function in the distribution of subjectivity and the staging of identity. One hears *MFA*, recognizes it, and experiences oneself as the kind of person that is "into" Eno—or IDM, or the avant-garde—and thereby finds a sense of belonging in the locale that mirrors one's self-understanding.

But something else might also happen. The performance of identity seems to derive from the fact that *MFA* is playing, not from any particular sound or assemblage of sounds on the album. Any bit that allows one to recognize "*MFA* is playing" will do the trick, which means that most of the differences in each sound's duration, texture, complexity, attack, or decay are irrelevant to the staging of an identity. I would thus distinguish a kind of listening where identities are staged from one that begins to surrender itself to the ambience of the work or the activities of the sounds therein (though one might move between both in a single listening). And I would intensify that distinction when the music begins to affect the kind of reverie that *MFA* occasionally induces. Once reverie sets in, one's situation dislodges, including one's manner of listening—it becomes salient and thus open to reflection, even interrogation. Not that one is brought into a world of pure sound. Instead, one finds oneself "always in the middle, between things, *intermezzo*," as the philosophers Gilles Deleuze and Félix Guattari put it.[48] So one isn't devoid of identity or a sense of self when reverie commences, but neither is one simply performing them either. Rather, one is encountering them. Such is the power of calm when curated by sounds that engage us but resolutely do not initiate and pursue a musical narrative.

CHAPTER 5

BETWEEN HEARING AND LISTENING

MUSIC FOR AIRPORTS *AS CONCEPTUAL ART*

> Very, very simple rules, clustering together, can produce very complex and actually rather beautiful results.
>
> —Eno, "Generative Music"

Music engages us in many ways. Beats may start us dancing; minor keys may make us sad. A work may programmatically depict the emotions of travelers at airports, or, more famously, each of the four seasons. It may also express emotions like sorrow, erotic or spiritual longing, or even outrage. Music may be formally inventive, showcasing facility with counterpoint, or be technically astonishing, demanding supreme virtuosity, which astonishes in turn. Or it might just be beautiful, offering us sounds where "pleasure is the law," as Debussy reportedly declared.[1]

MFA shows that music also operates ambiently. Engaging varied levels of attention, it moves between work, listener, and the sonic and social worlds where they meet. And even that movement presents us with more than one face: music as background, music for reverie, and music as immersive soundscape, staging the activity of sounds. But *MFA* also wears its compositional structure on its sleeve. In the absence of musical development, in its lack of technical virtuosity, one is led to wonder: How was this made, how does it hang together, and how should it be approached? In the distance that lies between it and what most listeners would expect, *MFA* poses questions, and in doing so it enters the realm of conceptual art.

Art becomes conceptual when it assesses its own occurrence relative to the concept "art." Marcel Duchamp's so-called *Fountain* (1917) and Andy Warhol's *Brillo Boxes* (1964) are so like ordinary objects that they appear like questions—or better still, questionable assertions. Viewing them, one hears: "This too is art."

Artworks also drift into the conceptual when they enact ideas. Lawrence Weiner's *Statements* (1968) pursues the point through descriptions of artworks. "One sheet of plywood secured to the floor or wall." "One standard dye marker thrown into the sea."[2] In the first example, an idea is conveyed: when plywood is hung as a painting or placed like a sculpture, it blurs the difference between the fine and useful arts, the beautiful and the mundane. But if the statement conveys the point, and as sufficiently as a work made with plywood, then a second claim is being made: art is often conceptual even when it is materially realized. The second example works toward similar ends.

Tying "standard dye marker" to "the sea" by way of the verb "thrown," it conveys a good deal if not everything to be had from following out such a procedure—quite a poor way to make one's mark.[3]

In Eno's art school days, concepts about art, the artist, and the audience were integral to his practice. *MFA* is no exception. Through what it negates and presents, concepts and ideas operate. Begin with "artist." It remains customary to think of artists expressing themselves emotionally through works—longing, sadness, anxiety, rage. *MFA* resists this kind of expression, beginning with the title, which directs us toward its function, "for airports," and away from its creator, who receives third billing: first *Ambient 1*, then *Music for Airports*, and finally *Brian Eno*. The names of the tracks, which only indicate their location on the album, also suggest that expressive content does not await the listener. And the music holds the line. The absence of appreciable dynamic contrast provides no sense of the ebb and flow of emotion. And the lack of musical development removes narrative structures that might indicate journeys, resolutions, or transformations. Instead, we have assemblages of sounds coming and going, resulting in textures. As we noted earlier, "2/1" offers recurring "ahhhhhs," but their compressed affect does not facilitate a sense of their state of mind or what induced them. Over time, particularly as the occasional synthesizer blends into their attack, they acquire a disembodied feel. They still sound like human voices, but without much expressive content; they are neither happy nor sad, hopeful nor distressed.

The absence of emotional expression might suggest that Eno has absented himself from these recordings. The manifesto he provides proves otherwise. While it functions like a program note, introducing listeners to what will befall them, the text also clarifies the character of the artist sending this our way. He refers to his "experiments" as well as his purposes, namely, to enrich the potential foreshortened by Muzak. Eno is thus fully operative in each track, but as a different kind of artist, one oriented toward conceptual enactment and social intervention rather than expression.

The character of Eno's artistic agency in *MFA* becomes more concrete if we return to the tracks. As we have observed, each has an assembled feel, tones layered atop one another, free from rhythmic and harmonic orders, and subjected to treatments like speed manipulation and compression. And while one hears recurring pianos in two of the tracks, the parts are short and detached from any display of learned musicianship. (No one is likely to think that Robert Wyatt gives a virtuoso performance on "1/1." And it took a while for anyone to even worry about who was singing with Eno on "2/1" and "1/2.")[4] The assembled feel, as if quasi-mechanical processes were operative, intensifies when we return to the "scores." They indicate that some pattern or procedure operates, but not one based on musical notation. In their lines, shades, and squiggles, Eno thus appears as a systems manipulator, organizing one system to intervene in another. (What else would we expect from a student of cybernetics?)

If you play with the iPad app Scape, which Eno designed with Peter Chilvers, you'll acquire a more concrete feel for this kind of "manipulation." The app provides one with a palette of tones, a tone series, and background sounds, each of which resounds in irregular ways. The sound patterns

FIGURE 5.1 Scape 1 made by the author

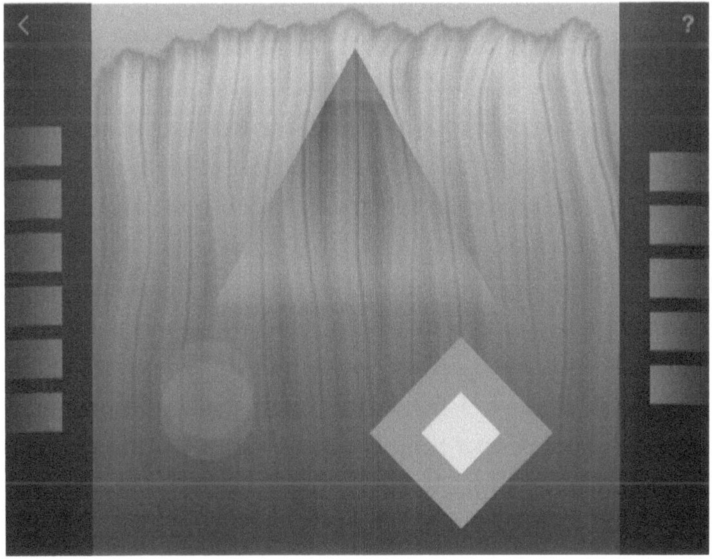

FIGURE 5.2 Scape 2 made by the author

are indicated by colors and shapes that one drags from the margins onto a plane (or canvas of sorts), arranging each spatially. One is also required to select a "mood button," which affects the overall sound and texture of the resulting composition. (One mood button correlates with crisp tones, another favors reverb.) Only one mood button operates in each scape, whereas more than one background and set of tones can be used simultaneously. Finally, one can save and replay the results.

If you proceed in the following way, the Eno-Chilvers app can establish one as a systems manipulator. Rather than trying to express an idea through the app (though you could), play with the system and generate patterns, preserving and modifying some, abandoning others. Follow its lead and guide its growth. And then deploy the results ambiently in different settings and through different equipment. And that's it: system manipulation and intervention. Granted, the app does most of the hard work; it generates tones, tone series, and treatments. And while dragging images across an iPad is nothing like working in a studio, Scape nevertheless gives one some experience of assembling or generating an electronic work built around the activity of sounds.

By embodying a certain conception of the artist, *MFA* also offers a conception of the artwork. Reich is again a principal influence. After encountering phase shifts in *It's Gonna Rain*, Reich became interested in "music as a gradual process," penning an essay with this title in 1968. Distinguishing himself from Cage, whose compositions often rely upon inaudible chance operations, Reich sought works whose insides were fully externalized—outside, as it were. "I am interested in perceptible processes," he wrote. "I want to be able to hear the process happening throughout the sounding music."[5]

Pendulum Music (1968) exemplifies Reich's program. Two, three, or four microphones should be suspended from a ceiling. Each is drawn and released so that it swings in front of or over a speaker connected to an amplifier to which the microphone is also connected. As it moves over the speaker, feedback occurs, increasing as the arc of the pendulum diminishes. "The piece is ended sometime after all mikes have come to a rest and are feeding back a continuous tone."[6]

The process organizing *Pendulum Music* is fully displayed, more or less: the proximity of the microphones to the speakers causes the feedback. Variety accrues relative to when each microphone passes over a speaker, and relative to which kinds of microphone, cable, amplifier, and speaker are being used, as well as to the location of the speakers (and listener) in the hall. And interactions among those variables provide each performance with a distinctive character. "Even when all the cards are on the table and everyone hears what is gradually happening in a musical process, there are still enough mysteries to satisfy all. These mysteries are the impersonal, unintended, psychoacoustic by-products of the intended process."[7]

In *MFA*, Eno seems more interested in accidental results than in fully displaying the processes that produce them. Discussing what he now terms "generative music," Eno reflected upon "2/1" and the voices he recorded in Conny Plank's studio. He explained that each of the loops involve a single-pitched "ahhhhh" repeated at temporal intervals

FIGURE 5.3 Steve Reich performing *Pendulum Music* at the Whitney Museum in 1969. Photograph by Richard Landry.

that make it very unlikely that recurring relations would result. When indicating the intervals (repeat every 23 1/2 seconds, every 25 7/8 seconds, every 29 15/16 seconds), he qualified each with an "or something," suggesting that their apparent precision is misleading, which it is.[8] As Eno noted in an earlier conversation with Cage, he did not determine the intervals of "2/1" ahead of time. Instead, he located the point on the tape where a note ended, and he cut the tape at a point that would introduce "a silence at least twice as long as the sound. So I'd spin off a whole lot of extra tape and then cut loops."[9] The arbitrariness of Eno's snips is essential to the piece, however. "It wasn't measured," he says. "And I didn't want to measure it, because I did want to arrive at complicated rather than simple relationships."[10] And by "complicated," he means irregular, even asynchronous as far as the track is concerned. Speaking again about "2/1," he says: "What I mean is they all repeat in cycles that are called incommensurable—they are not likely to come back into sync again." And he goes on to say, speaking more generally and indicating the idea embodied by generative music, "Very, very simple rules clustering together, can produce very complex and actually rather beautiful results."[11]

This aversion to formal simplicity (or unity) also seems to distinguish generative music from John White's *Machine Music*, some of which Eno produced on Obscure 8 (1978). White termed various pieces "machines" because they adhered to fixed rules. "I use the word Machine to define a consistent process governing a series of actions within a particular sound world."[12] Such consistency led Brian Dennis to claim: "John White has rationalized indeterminacy, and has replaced both musical argument and musical accident with the almost tangible relentless object."[13] While *MFA* never becomes an object of this order, neither does it exemplify either complete indeterminacy or musical argument. Instead, it conspires with indeterminacy by experimenting with something short of a fully rationalized compositional process.

In the context of conceptual art, therefore, *MFA* has its own points to make. Like *Pendulum Music*, it objectifies an impersonal process, which enacts an idea—musical works can be organized by processes other than artistic genius or the mastery of compositional technique. But Eno's tracks do so without rendering the logic of that process fully apparent. Does this render *MFA* less rigorous than *Pendulum Music*, at least with regard to Reich's founding idea? I think not. Something else drives what we might term Eno's preference for effects over causes. As Reich himself notes, the eventual sounds of a piece like *Pendulum Music* are bound to forces not of his making: the room, the character of the microphones and speakers, the relative position of the listener, his or her discernments, and so on. In a very thorough way, therefore, *Pendulum Music* results from processes that are opaque to their creator. The work is thus a result of interactions among intended and unintended processes, and that is precisely the conception of the work exemplified by *MFA*. To be clear, I am not suggesting that Reich somehow imagines his work to be fully autonomous. What I am claiming is that Eno's willingness to rely upon "hidden structural devices," to use Reich's language, is not due to a lack of rigor but to his conception of the artwork and artist. And that conception highlights the inevitable surrender of creativity and control to a network of forces (or processes) that enable artworks to do what they do. As Eno tells Ian MacDonald, "Well, all systems have their peculiar orientation and direction. The whole problem is one of 'How much drift do I want and how much direction do I want?' "[14]

Eno's conception of "generative music" also proposes a particular conception of art. A brief return to the sonic turn will clarify what I mean. Recall that many contributors to the sonic turn wished to open music to the sounds of the world. The recurring thought was that nature—or the cosmos, more broadly—had more to offer by way of sound than the European tradition and its instruments could capture. At one extreme, futurists like Russolo tried to humanize those sounds, creating compositions that strove to translate the sounds of the world into an expanded but nevertheless fully realized musical idiom. At the other extreme, Cage sought to let sounds be sounds through compositions that removed as thoroughly as possible his taste, judgment, and skill as a composer.

When interpreted conceptually, the approaches of Russolo and Cage create an opposition: either (a) art absorbs nature in a self-enlarging process, versus (b) art exposes nature in a self-effacing one. The former offers us culture over nature, whereas the latter labors to displace human activity from an emerging culture—or field—of sounds. *MFA* eludes this opposition, seeking neither a denatured culture nor an ascetically cleansed field of sounds. Instead, it enacts itself as one aspect of the world operating on another. By working with its world, and by clarifying itself with theories that naturalize the human desire to make art, it presents itself as nature unfolding, taking nature, cybernetically, as a dynamic system of interactions that includes its (and our) own efforts.

In a talk from 2011, Eno invoked gardening while explaining his approach to composition. "I suppose my feeling about gardening . . . is that what one is doing is working in collaboration with the complex and unpredictable processes of nature. And trying to insert into that some inputs that will take advantage of those processes."[15] Simply in its conception of ambience, *MFA* enacts this idea. Rather than replacing the sonic field with a musical work, *MFA* interacts dynamically (and unpredictably) with every scene it enters. But various features of the album also exemplify analogous conceptions of art and nature that generate variety through the interaction of systems or patterns. "2/1" fades into view, as if coming from afar. It does not begin at the beginning, in other words. (None of the tracks do, in fact, if we consult their "scores," which indicate that Eno has constructed the album from larger sonic chains.)

As it underscores that it belongs to a longer series or flow of time, "2/1" is nothing short of ecological: voices overlay others and develop a temporary but singular character through those interactions. This idea may be clearer at a content level in tracks like "Lantern Marsh" from *On Land*, but a similar arrangement is indicated by the partially unscripted relations among the sounds that assemble and give way in "2/1." Each loop has a character and logic of its own, but the whole results from unplanned interactions, which offer us a way of thinking dynamic systems like marshes, city traffic, or the long history of a town like Woodbridge, where Eno was born.

Our focus on the generative logic of particular tracks should not obscure the full breadth of the conceptualization enacted by *MFA*. Other variables are marked by the album and thus drawn into the generative scene. Alongside its internal interactions, it also implicates the artist, as we have seen. She or he manipulates, that is, intervenes into operative processes, a harnesser of currents rather than a creator ex nihilo. But the listener is also implicated. Because *MFA* does not enforce or sustain any particular mode of attention, the work leads the listener to encounter his or her own hearing. And in that encounter, one realizes that the sonic character (and function) of the work shifts with shifts in attention as well as with changes in how the music is reproduced. The ecology presented by *MFA* is thus remarkably expansive: the work, the artist, the listener, and the various technologies and resonant environments integral to each occurrence of the work. *MFA* thus enacts a rich idea of eco-cultural history. And I want to stress my use of the word "enacts." "2/1" is not just a symbol of how nature and culture unfold over time and generate variety. It too belongs to that process, and it presents itself as such. It thus enacts or dramatizes the idea. Listening to it, one is confronted with a multivariable, dynamic process that envelops us even as we contribute to it. It is not exclusively the fruit of Eno's imagination, the systems he deploys, the place it resounds, or what we, as listeners, make of it. And in underscoring this with sounds and words, it enacts an idea of codependent, temporal processes, resonating as a music of the world.

By situating human activity within the world that it relies upon and shapes, *MFA* also helps us to rethink the "activity of sounds." When an album is playing or people are performing, the so-called activity of sounds includes the activity of persons, directly in the case of performers, indirectly in the case of technologies. (Humans not only made these technologies, they also operate them.) We have yet another reason to hesitate before Cage's suggestion that a "sound is a sound and a man is a man." Humans make sounds and do not cease to be human in that making—one becomes a piano *player*, or we become *performers* in an avant-garde piece, turning dials on radios in accord with a score compiled by someone else. Similarly, many sounds, particularly in the context of music, are not freestanding events but results of human undertakings. Yes, those sounds may not entail expression or convey programmatic content. But they would not occur without that undertaking, and so even when a piece can be said to insist "This is just sound," it remains bound to human agency. It thus seems a mistake, particularly in the context of music, to pry apart the activity of sounds and the activity of those integral to their making.[16]

While *MFA* enacts an ecology of interactions, one interaction is indicated more than it is conceptualized: listening. When *MFA* plays, many wonder: How should I listen to this? And because the album rarely if ever sustains attention, one is often left hearing one's listening, so to speak. Not that *MFA* enacts an idea of listening (except insofar as its composer is also a listener to his own generative processes). Rather, it provokes reflection on listening, and determinately. Open to a variety of attentions, *MFA* allows one to encounter one's listening in various ways.

But before we explore listening in the context of *MFA*, let us briefly tour Eno's experiments in visual art, which pursue many of the same conceptual points we have just entertained. In fact, the 1986 installation *Living Room* contains a pun that conveys its ambient function as well as the conceptual enactment we just discussed. The place his light works bathe is a dynamic (or living) system of processes, which results in a location where one, for the time being, can reside. Derived from interactions among fifteen "independently programmed cycles of colored light," the work was organized to "create the gradations of color in the piece," which unfolded slowly over time. As Eno says, conjoining his creative arenas: "My music and videos do change, but they change slowly. And they change in such a way that doesn't matter if you miss a bit. I try to make installations a place to sit awhile."[17]

As Brian Dillon has noted, the seven parts of the video project *Mistaken Memories of Medieval Manhattan* (1980–81) also enact Eno's program.[18] Each part was taken from film gathered by a video camera set on its side and allowed to film whatever came into view. The parts selected by Eno

FIGURE 5.4 A cover of *Art Forum* in 1986

show various cityscapes that juxtapose the stasis of the skyline with a moving sky that introduces shifts in light. In a very straightforward way, each is thus a "motion picture." And while the content is ostensibly more determinate than *Living Room*—New York, buildings, clouds, etc.—in the end, the subject matter is much the same. "What you see is simply light patterned in various ways," as Eno says.[19] (▶ Video 5.1 contains a clip from *mistaken memories of manhattan*) And this is accentuated by the odd perspective of the camera—the buildings are all pushed to the right margin, leaving the bulk of the frame to the sky and emphasizing that these "buildings" are dark shapes, at least as far as the motion picture is concerned.

Similar ideas operate on *MFA*'s front cover. Abstract at first glance, it appears to be a close-up of a map or portion of a map. It charts a few lakes and several rivers as well as their forks, with lower elevations marked in green. (Or are they forested areas around most of the water?) One also might take the cover to offer an airplane view, but the image is clearly assembled from Ben-Day dots, like one of Roy Lichtenstein's comic strip paintings. What first seemed an aerial view proves instead to be shaded colors and lines; and what might be lower elevations (or "forests") are, at base, assembled spaces of green, as well as ten or so whitish spots whose landscape referent is oblique at best. In other words, what you see on the cover "is light patterned in various ways."

It is difficult not to think of the "activity of sounds" when reading and/or viewing "light patterned in various ways." And given that Eno is subjecting the light to various treatments, say by occasionally adjusting the color of the image or by making the camera exceptionally light sensitive to accentuate subtle changes, Eno seems to be approaching his sonic and visual material in similar ways.[20] In the liner notes to *Brian Eno: 14 Paintings*, a DVD containing

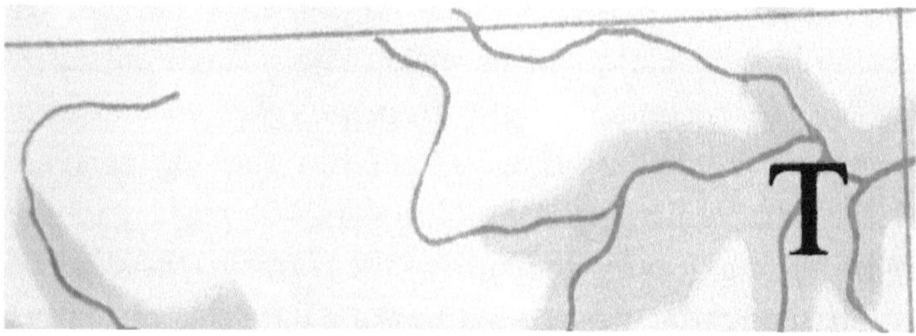

FIGURE 5.5 A detail of the right corner of the *MFA* album cover

Mistaken Memories, Eno even draws a parallel between his manipulations of the camera's light sensitivity to the use of an "expander" in the studio, which lowers the volume of the quietest tones and increases the volume of louder ones, thus amplifying the track's dynamic range. Intriguingly, therefore, Eno found it easy to move not only from the visual arts to music while a young man in art school but from music to the visual arts as an established figure in the world of music.

Mistaken Memories also sparks interest because it employs tracks from *MFA* ("1/2") and *On Land*. Moreover, it does so in ways that allow Eno's two generative systems, the sonic and the visual, to dovetail conceptually and to provide each other with a different but complementary ambient presence. (If ambient music provides a metaphorical "tint," why not add a literal one?) The difference lies in the fact that one needs to look at the screen to view it, whereas sound can audibly fill a room no matter where one looks. And this makes the motion pictures in *Mistaken Memories* less likely to function as a visual background to other activities, particularly if one wants to witness and admire the "light patterned in various ways." The video work thus seems more immersive than work that operates only sonically, and this may be why immersive soundscapes like those from *On Land* accompany six of the seven motion pictures.

We have returned to the question of listening and how it unfolds in the presence of *MFA*.[21] Let us now recount the various ways in which one might listen to *MFA*, but with the following caveat. I have zero interest in assigning, categorically, kinds of music to kinds of listening. Whether one kind of listening finds purchase with a given work rests on particular listeners and what they are able to hear and report.

As we have observed on more than one occasion, *MFA* settles easily into background music. Lacking significant dynamic variation and avoiding melodic development, it easily accompanies other activities such as cleaning up, chatting, or writing. *Background listening* is thus one kind of listening (or hearing) available to those who engage *MFA*. When listening in this way, we do not try to grasp the whole of a track, let alone the album, nor do we scrutinize how various elements relate to one another. We probably don't concentrate on the activity of sounds, beyond giving it some passing notice. Instead, we let bits and pieces of the sound drift into our awareness, and not in accord with any recurring rules, as we would if we were listening for harmonic relations or motivic development.

Recall, in contrast, Kassabian's conception of *ubiquitous listening*. Her suggestion is that we are often involved in background listening, and usually in response to unelected sonic material. In fact, she argues that background listening may be the most common way in which people encounter music, even among those people who listen in other ways as well. If she is right, and I think she may be (at least in several industrial contexts), it is worth our time to think more about what transpires with background listening. As Christopher Case, a Muzak designer, suggests: "Now it's not cut and dry, whether you listen or don't. It [Muzak] is just something that doesn't interfere. To think that people don't listen is stupid. People are listening."[22]

In a world of diminishing privacy, it is difficult not to align background listening with subliminal influence and, when the sonic material is standardized, with the homogenization of taste. And no doubt, these are legitimate concerns, as are the ways in which background music can surreptitiously create conditions of welcome, obliviousness, or hostility for various persons. But "influence" can run in more than one direction, and where there is a risk, there is also an opportunity. Knowing how background music helps establish moods, which in turn enable or interrupt other pursuits, allows one to curate and individuate one's contexts. And that makes *MFA*'s ability to induce reverie all the more intriguing. If calm and a space to think seem hard to find, we know of at least one album that can buck that trend (albeit gently).

As the name indicates, "background listening" involves a pair of concepts that establish a continuum. Its partner would be something like "foreground listening," though I would prefer to think in terms of *performance listening*. (Listening intently to a musical performance seems like the paradigmatic example of focusing one's attention on explicitly foregrounded sounds while purposefully ignoring rival and ambient sounds.) Performance listening, as I understand it, involves one's full and learned concentration on a sonic event, whether in a concert hall or in the sound field instituted by a home stereo or headphones. (Full concentration is at least the ideal of this activity, even if it rarely if ever proves possible in practice.) In such cases, one very well may listen for the ways in which parts interact to form a whole larger than their sum, and the more one hears some interactions, the better one can be said to listen in this manner.

Note, however, that one might also concentrate on the activity of sounds in La Monte Young's *Composition 1960 #7*, attending to the overtones at work, and with the help of insights from harmonic theory, psychoacoustics, and so on. Or one might follow the reverberations of "Balloon Payment," an initially startling if brief piece by the Deep Listening Band. In the latter case, because so many traditional musical orders are absent, one must find other things to focus upon, such as the relative duration of the tone and its attack and decay as well as its micro-dynamics, which persist as it endures. Or one's listening might concentrate on the sounds and the situation that generates it. Annea Lockwood's early compositions explored the kind of sounds that glass can make. *Wine Glass* (1970) presents one with the activity of sounds from an object manipulated by a person in a room, and one can focus on the relative complexity of the result, catching reverb, micro-dynamics, something like timbre. In short, while one normally doesn't think of performance listening within the sonic turn, something very much like it seems possible, perhaps even solicited at points. (Recall that Young speaks of trying to get "inside a sound.")

Joanna Demers has conceptualized a kind of listening that moves between background listening and attention to the activity of sounds, particularly as they arise from something other than traditional instruments and music practices. Such an approach "heeds intermittent moments of a work without searching for a trajectory that unites such moments" and appreciates the "characteristics of nonmusical sound as aesthetic objects."[23] This approach—she terms it *aesthetic listening*—captures precisely the kind of interactions that *MFA* involves when operating ambiently. But she also sees it operating well beyond the confines of music that, like *MFA*, lacks a unifying logic and explicitly situates itself at points of interaction between organized sounds and the world in which they resonate. In fact, as she describes it, aesthetic listening simply listens to whatever the listener feels like—"We may choose to attend to development, or else we may pay only intermittent attention to sound while also attending to other sensory phenomena."[24] I find this too diffuse to amount to a distinct kind of listening. Instead, it seems like a broad awareness that moves between various kinds of sensuous perceptions: sound, sight, touch, possibly smell or taste, and potentially any of these in some synesthetic combination. Such a general aesthetic sensibility may be a praiseworthy project. And no doubt, a feast awaits anyone who pursues it. But it seems too broad to stand as a kind of listening in itself.

Demer's notion of aesthetic listening worries me in another way. Focused on its own preferences and whimsy, it seems to willfully ignore the sound source and any logic organizing it, and that seems like a refusal to listen rather than a kind of listening. *MFA* gives itself to background listening and actively resists those who search it for rhythms, harmonies, and melodic development. In fact, when we approach it from the standpoint of performance listening, it almost always eludes us. And if one then turns to thoughts that arise in the calm it induces, one is nevertheless engaging the album on terms responsive to its character. That would entail *adequate listening*, in Ola Stockfelt's sense: one knows the genre and what aspects of the sonic event it accentuates and develops.[25] Because works present themselves in various ways, one would expect and want various ways of listening. But each way of listening should be somewhat responsive to the sonic event being performed or reproduced. Otherwise, it will prove difficult to distinguish listening to something from ignoring it. (Imagine only listening to the timbre of my voice as I ask you a question.)

Admittedly, my caution is conservative. It wishes to conserve the idea that musical works have a character of their own, which a listener should strive to ascertain and appreciate, even if one eventually finds it lacking in one respect or another. (I hope this study has been an exercise in listening of this kind. *MFA* is an unusual record, and I have tried to register how, why, and what its unusualness makes possible for those who take it seriously, which can involve allowing it to function as background music.) But maybe my approach is not conservative enough. By admitting into the world of "music" an album like *MFA*, are we not giving in to a culture that increasingly invites people to listen distractedly? Doesn't *MFA* contribute to conditions that bring about what the philosopher Theodor Adorno has termed *regressive listening*?[26]

One listens regressively, Adorno thinks, when one listens in a fragmentary way but still believes one is engaging a work. And this is particularly common, he finds, when association with that work grants some non-musical value such as prestige. One thereby appears "cultured" or hip. While Adorno has the fate of composers like Beethoven in mind, others know a similar phenomenon in less erudite contexts. Many committed rock fans complain about "scenesters," those who come less to listen than to be seen attending the show. Regardless, in both cases, the result is that one never tries to apprehend the work in any concrete manner—in other words, one does not attend to the elements and relationships that give the work its character. At best, one latches on to isolated parts, as if they carried the whole, which is why Adorno speaks of fetishistic listening as a dimension of regressive listening.

When fetishistic approaches become the rule, listeners lose the ability to concentrate on and follow concrete musical material. They may even deny, Adorno fears, that others can and do listen to works as integrated wholes. Instead, they listen atomistically and dissociatively, that is, to parts in isolation. And again, one could extend this concern beyond the concert hall. Many ignore rock lyrics, whereas others listen to them and only them. Some focus on guitar tones and ignore the rhythm section altogether. And many are wowed by instrumental virtuosity, independent of any other features of the work. In these cases, something like "regressive listening" seems operative.

I find Adorno's concern well placed, although I would extend it to music that he would refuse to take seriously, either because of its compositional simplicity or derivative status, or even because of its spontaneous character. I share the concern because when we listen regressively, we lose our ability to know and benefit from a history of artistic achievement. Moreover, disinterest in the specificity of musical events undermines our ability to expand our knowledge of music lying outside the canon that has gathered around composers like Bach, Beethoven, Chopin, Stravinsky, and Schoenberg. Listening habits that only attend to their own fluctuating affections are narcissistic rather than responsive. The object is only an occasion for another self-relation, which is quite different from familiarizing oneself with and learning from the creative strivings of others. (In fact, I prefer *narcissistic listening* to "regressive listening." The former further specifies the fault, and it avoids any sense that "performance listening," which Adorno champions, is somehow progressive.)

If we return to *MFA*, I don't find it operating in support of regressive listening. It is not presented as somehow operating according to the true essence of music, such that one grasps the core of all or most music when one grasps what occurs in *MFA*. "Generative music" names only one compositional approach. And *MFA*'s ostensible function, to operate ambiently, does not purport to rival music that establishes a clear hierarchy of attention, with performance listening at the top. Anyone who listens and reads, and the album asks us to do both, should recognize *MFA* as just one way to introduce music into various social settings, particularly those outside performance spaces. And it does not need to negate more traditional musical offerings to make room for itself and what it induces. If anything, it happily seeks out spaces more appropriate to its ambient efforts, namely, homes and their various rooms, thus leaving performance music and listening to the kind of experiences they better realize. Moreover, it avoids one trap that has afflicted avant-garde efforts to return art to everyday life, namely, an embrace of rather unlifelike performance practices and performance spaces.[27]

Humility is not all that keeps *MFA* from contributing to the rise of regressive listening. By operating in various registers—as background music, as music for reverie, and as conceptual art—*MFA* solicits yet another kind of listening, one that begins with the question "How should I approach a work that seems to require multiple approaches?" Because its distracted awareness will miss the album's conceptual enactments as well as its attention to the activity of sounds and its ability to induce reverie, regressive or narcissistic listening will remain unresponsive to a great deal that *MFA* offers. Yes, a distracted awareness is compatible with the album's background function, but even then, the history and logic of that intervention, including Eno's remarks about it, will probably elude a genuinely distracted listener. It seems, therefore, that multiple facets of *MFA* run counter to the trends that entrench narcissistic listening. In fact, the album's manifold character seems to require a kind of listening that we have yet to discuss.

Prisms work by refracting the light we normally look through as we attend to objects and landscapes. Dispersive prisms refract light in a way that reveals spectral colors that the eye overlooks in a light-filled room or during the day. It's as if the spectral prism engages light in a way that allows its complexity to appear. I think *MFA* requires a listening that has a similar effect. To be clear, the goal is not a listening that can somehow engage all of *MFA*'s multiple dimensions simultaneously. I don't think that's possible (and that would just be a kind of adequate listening). One cannot let *MFA* function as background music and scrutinize the activity of its sounds, though one might let it operate ambiently as one considers its conceptual enactment. But even then, if the album induces reverie, one's considerations will be interrupted, and one will be suspended between hearing and listening. The album thus requires a *prismatic listening* that knows it needs to partition the work into various dimensions and attend to each, which requires a listening that knows the genre but is also capable of hearing particularities, especially where the activity of sounds is concerned.

Not that *MFA* rewards all kinds of listening. It does not seem to facilitate what we might call *immersive listening*: full absorption into a sonic event at more than a self-conscious level. It is perhaps too gentle and certainly too asynchronous, though I suppose one could work on remaining attentive to how the tones interact with one's listening situation and thus immerse oneself in its ambient character, even experimenting with how it resounds in different resonant environments. But even then, other music seems better suited to immersive listening.

"Deep listening," which we have already discussed, is the paradigmatic example of immersive listening, but it brings with it a whole series of concerns that one needn't share to register the many ways that sound envelops us. It thus makes sense to imagine a broader category that can account for aligned but distinct approaches to music. One kind of post-rock relies on extended pieces that feature stark dynamics, heightened-to-extreme volumes, rich instrumental textures within simple melodic phrases, and underscored, accelerating rhythms, all working toward a clear crescendo. (If *MFA* leaves narrative behind, post-rock of this stripe epically embraces it.) "Christmas Steps" (1999) by the Scottish band Mogwai combines these elements in a totally absorbing, even transporting manner. Heard at a suitable volume—loud—it is difficult not to be fully immersed in the music, feeling the bass in your chest (say around 4′00″) and much of the rest with your body, say by bobbing your head to a guitar line (pick one up around 3′00″ and stay with its move into double time by 4′25″) or swaying your torso and moving your arms (say, to keep with the five-note bassline and drum interplay that commences around 4′40″) (▶ Audio 5.1). But this needn't involve what Oliveros terms "global attention," which aims to "take in the whole of the space/time continuum of sound," and yet, like deep listening, it seems immersive.[28]

What about *performance listening*, which privileges self-conscious scrutiny of the music's sonic character? Earlier we noted that one could attend to the activity of sounds in this manner, but our examples were La Monte Young and the Deep Listening Band. (If you are wondering what distinguishes performance listening from immersive listening, it's the former's narrower field of attention.) What does *MFA* disclose when scrutinized in this way? Along the way we have already encountered the voices in "2/1" and how the synthesizer interacts with them. We have also discussed the compressed attack and decay of the synthetic horns on "2/2." And we have observed, more generally, how the absence of rhythm removes a certain kind of anticipation from one's attention, which leaves one more at the mercy of whatever enters one's sonic horizon, and for however long it lingers. But let us not forget that the activity of sounds is bound to other activities. Let me suggest an exercise, therefore, that might intensify our experience of the sounds activated by *MFA*.

The sounds of *MFA* are usually bound to some mode of stereo reproduction. But what happens to the sounds when these modes shift. say, from a vinyl source in a stationary stereo system to a CD in the same system to earbuds connected to a portable playback device to a Bluetooth player in a car? If we were listening for more traditional European classical musical orders, such shifts probably wouldn't prove that significant, presuming we were listening to the same performance. The motifs would be developed in more or less the same way, and the harmonic relations employed would remain quite consistent. But when the issue is the activity of sounds, material differences prove to be quite material.

Let's work with "2/2," which deploys synthesizer tones and is a purely electronic piece. I'll begin with a CD played through a two-channel stereo system. As noted, the piece is built around the coming and going of hornlike tones. They are hornlike because in their attack their envelope opens and closes somewhat quickly. That said, the attack lacks the brassy brightness, even bite of an actual horn, and none of the transient qualities of an actual horn are present, such as the push of breath propelling the sound. The sound is thus only hornlike in a general way.

The groupings of sounds also offer little by way of texture. As they sustain, one doesn't hear much by way of microdynamics. They seem compressed in that regard, and one struggles to get inside them. Instead, one's attention moves to new tones entering the sonic horizon. Certain sustained low tones are exceptions. As they linger, they introduce a gentle dissonance, whereas others rumble and resonate, morphing slightly.

The action, such as it is, lies more with how the sounds interact, but even here one senses juxtapositions and overlays more than interactions producing overtones. The work seems very painterly in that regard, as if the track were a motion picture, sounds coming into and exiting a foreground, an experience heightened by the three-dimensional, stereographic image conjured by the stereo. This sense of a scene of emergence is heightened by the occasional ascent or descent of short musical phrases, usually no longer than three notes. And because they occur outside any melodic development, the spatiality of "ascent" and "descent" is apropos.

On the whole, then, "2/2," played back from a CD on a two-channel stereo, presents sounds in a very painterly fashion. One can focus on the hornlike envelope of the tones, but they do not offer very much by way of texture, and they are so like one another that the whole asserts itself over the parts. Attacks and decays can be felt and traced, but a dense, generative center repeatedly claims one's attention.

Before we move to LP, we should be clear about what our exercise shows. There isn't a stable "text," as it were, lurking behind what we are hearing. *MFA* is just its sounds committed to tape. Without a score lying behind them, and given its embrace of variety through accidental interaction, we shouldn't wonder which stereo reproduction is the *real* work. (I suppose we might if the album was made for a specific combination of turntable, amplifier, and speaker, but it wasn't.) Instead, our concern should be the activity of sounds as they vary across different reproduction systems.

If we move to LP, maintaining the same playback system, the painterly quality of "2/2" intensifies even as the parts individuate. One could say that the tones have greater textural depth, particularly the lower tones, although the attack of the higher tones is increased as well, which allows them to burst a bit into musical space. More generally, each tone's envelope opens more gradually, and the reverb operating is more audible. One has more opportunities to listen in to the sounds unfolding, therefore. They remain compressed, but their occurrence brings greater differentiation over time.

On LP, the decay is underscored on all tones, and that allows one to hear them lose their pitch as they fade, which presents dissonances that never resolve. But that dissonance doesn't fracture the track either. Instead, it gives one a deeper sense of sounds emerging and passing away, which intensifies even further in the LP's deeper and broader stereo image. A kind of kinetic, three-dimensional sound sculpture unfolds on LP, therefore, even if the compression means it never quite shimmers.

One could listen to other formats. Headphones might further highlight textures, for example. But there seems little reason to pursue that here—the point has been made. Having been led by *MFA*'s conceptual enactment to bind the activity of sounds to whatever (and whoever) makes them, we now know that *MFA* can provide a shifting palette of sounds for those wanting to focus on their comings and goings. And this suggests that a kind of uniqueness can be found outside the context of singular performances, Cage's antipathy toward recordings notwithstanding. As David Grubbs observes, recordings, like photographs, preserve the accidental and unintended, and he concludes that "recording comes to us as a means of representing this extra-compositional excess that is crucial to, for lack of a better term, music."[29] While I agree, my point here is that each playback could be something of a "performance" given changes in media, playback technology, room conditions, and so on.

What would happen, however, if *MFA* were scored for and performed by musicians playing instruments? What then confronts us when we press play? I have in mind the work of Bang on a Can, a contemporary music organization founded in 1987 by Michael Gordon, David Lang, and Julia Wolfe, which was soon joined by Evan Ziporyn, who cofounded the associated performance ensemble, Bang on a Can All-Stars, in 1992. The group came together in a commitment to program and perform music that was innovative regardless of its classification—avant-garde, pop, uptown, downtown, etc.[30]

In 1998, Band on a Can released a studio recording of *MFA*, with each member assuming responsibility for one track.[31] The thought was that *MFA* "deserves to be listened to like you'd listen to a great piece of music."[32] While the tracks are instantly recognizable, their sonic feel and musical character are appreciably different, and because new relationships are introduced, the conceptual character of the work also shifts (▶ Audio 5.2).

Let's stay with "2/2," which Ziporyn scored and arranged. With an ear for the activity of sounds, one finds oneself in a very different soundscape. The compressed palette of the album track gives way to sounds that are as various as the instruments used to produce them. At the outset, the barely pulsing drone from the album is replaced by a rich, sonorous overplay of acoustic bass and bass clarinet, carrying the same pitch. Moreover, the breath, conspicuously

FIGURE 5.6 The Bang on a Can All Stars performing *MFA*. Photo by Kenny Savelson/Bang on a Can.

absent from the hornlike tones on the album, seems audible underneath the slow scrape of the bow. More generally, the sounds one hears are clearly those of instruments such as a cello and violin. Not that the average listener will recognize every instrument playing. (I only know that a guitar is treated with an EBow device because Ziporyn indicated this in correspondence.) But recognizing even a few instruments and growing accustomed to their tone and the timbre of their interactions displaces the monochromatic character of the album track. In fact, what is a displacement on the one hand is a placement on the other. Each instrument has a kind of individual resonance missing on the original version of "2/2." The sculptural density of the album thus gives way to clear interactions among instruments and players. The result is thus more like the ecology of "Lantern Marsh"—a sense of life blows through the whole track, and not just from the clarinet parts.

Not just the overall texture and spatiality of "2/2" shifts in the Bang on a Can rendition. The instrumental arrangement bursts with feeling at points. Once abstract assemblages now seem full of longing, such as when what sounds like a cello, violin, and horn overlap between 2′46″ and 2′58″. Eno himself observes how, in the presence of persons (either directly or through a recording, I would add), various tones and tonal groupings brim with emotion.[33] The soundscape of Bang on a Can's "2/2" is thus not only enlivened but humanized, particularly around 4′40″ when the clarinet begins to improvise after a scene-setting introduction by the pipa (▶ Audio 5.3). The appearance of frank, individualized expression therefore brings a distinct inhabitant to the soundscape. And the sense that this scene is inhabited only deepens when the clarinet and pipa enter conversation. But what else would one expect when the activity of these sounds springs directly from the activity of people playing together, and playing a score arranged such that they, in particular, could play together?[34]

Other changes are apparent as well. With a second section of improvising and a concluding section full of quickly strummed mandolin tones, sustained EBow guitar chords, and drawn out tones from the bass and a horn or two, there are no less than four parts, and no doubt a more refined ear might make sharper demarcations. Ziporyn's arrangement thus draws a narrative out of the album track that I doubt I would have found if I had never heard Bang on a Can's version.[35] Nor would I have taken the whole album

FIGURE 5.7 Evan Ziporyn. Photo by Christine Southworth.

as symphonic, replete with movements, as Bang on a Can does. (As I noted at the beginning, names like "1/1," "1/2," "2/1," and "2/2" seem to direct one toward a less integrated listening experience—not exclusively, but no one would be mistaken to take each track on its own terms.) Finally, the non-musician is hard if not impossible to find in what Bang on a Can achieves, particularly in the mesmerizing improvisations in "2/2." These are elite performers, and one listens for intonation, interplay, and expressiveness in ways that seem out of step with what the LP assembles.

As *MFA*'s organization and sonic character change in the hands of Bang on a Can, so does its conceptual enactment. Listening to the work presented by Bang on a Can, one encounters an interpretation and a performance, and thereby a more traditional pattern of musical art. The decisive change is less the move from album to concert hall than Eno's emergence as something like a traditional composer. Where the studio impresario once worked, there stands the author of a score that functions as instructions for performers (although in this case the score is the album itself). And that, in turn, pulls the work away from generative music, at least as Eno practices it. The generative system and its unintended variety ceases to operate when its results are scored as pitches that performers reproduce. Through Bang on a Can's interpretations, the music thus becomes Eno's in a way that it isn't on the album.[36]

In its new guise, one wonders what befalls *MFA*'s ambient character. With so much to listen to—performers, instruments, and the interpretation—there is more to absorb one's attention, particularly if one begins to track narrative trajectories in and across tracks. Not that it can't function ambiently or induce the kind of reverie we discussed. But there is a good bit more to absorb the listener, particularly if she or he is musically trained, and that seems to leave us with a more traditional sense of musical art than the album provides. The music now seems to invite (if not quite enforce) performance listening. Recall Michael Gordon's reason for programming it—*MFA* "deserves to be listened to like you'd listen to a great piece of music."

Amid these shifts at the conceptual level, one issue bears special notice. *MFA*'s cybernetic cast, which is evident in its ambient function and generative character, stages conditions for its own reception and interpretation. There is an accidental quality to *MFA*—a few snips at different points on the tape, a longer playing time, and we would have had a different album, even though the basic concept of the work would have remained the same. (Eno sometimes mentions the existence of other versions of "2/1.")[37] *MFA* thus opens itself to interpretation in ways that more canonical works do not. (It would be strange to try and "get right" a piece that seeks variety through a combination of selection and chance.) As a cybernetic intervention into extant systems, *MFA* thus invites the favor in return, whether one varies the playback system, interplays copies of the album, or hands scored moments off to players of exquisite feeling and skill. The Bang on a Can renditions thus extend the experiment in variety that *MFA* initiated when Eno began assembling, treating, and looping bits and pieces of source material. He sought results he could not anticipate. And now those unforeseen results have generated their own unforeseen results in a broader cybernetic system involving performers, arrangers, and audience members, as well as the original album, which now has to resound alongside a partner of sorts.

CROSSROADS

AN AFTERWORD

Tape awaits composers who can use it sensitively.
—Roger Maren, "Music by Montage and Mixing"

Some will think I've overstated the achievement of *MFA*, just as many, including collaborators, were put off by Eno's purported non-musicianship. Jon Hassell, with whom Eno made *Possible Musics: Fourth World Vol. 1* (1980), seems almost dismissive when recalling the collaboration. "I knew he's an art school graduate so he doesn't really play an instrument basically, and so his contributions were in bringing the art school mind to the studio. . . . For instance, turning the tape over and getting the backwards echo."[1] The idea that "he doesn't play anything" is a common refrain. Bryan Ferry has remarked: "You see, Eno is a very clever fellow, but he's not really a musician. He doesn't know how to play anything."[2] I see the point, as far as it goes. An album like *MFA* offers neither virtuoso performances nor compositional ingenuity, at least not in any traditional sense. On those scores, it remains odd and underwhelming, and one might think: What's the fuss? Eno himself has observed: "If you're not in the manipulative mode anymore you're not quite sure actually how to measure your own contribution; if you're not constructing things and pushing things in a certain direction and working towards goals, what is your function?"[3]

But is there more to hear and consider in the presence of music than the virtuoso manipulations of traditional composers and performers? Yes, I've been arguing, while trying to render legible (or audible) what that "more" involves. And to be clear, one can appreciate that "more" without supposing that *MFA* displaces other objects of musical affection. The "doesn't play anything" point is therefore odd. What mistake is it correcting? What confusion does it clarify? Is the fear that listeners will think "Forget Bach, there is Brian." "Hendrix? We have snake guitar!" Does *MFA* lead one toward such proclamations? If anything, it seems studious in its restraint. Its rival is Muzak. In the context of music history, therefore, *MFA* resounds as it does in a living room. It invites rather than enforces attention, and it leaves plenty of room for other projects.

Perhaps the worry is, while disarmingly inviting, even charming, *MFA* is too simple to merit sustained attention and reflection. But *MFA* offers its own rewards. Those who engage it find four musically simple tracks and a complex, multifaceted artwork that offers listeners several points of entry. One can listen to the activities of the sounds it produces. Or one can allow it to hover in the background, though it might not remain there. In fact, one might find oneself surrendering to a reverie induced by its dynamically limited, arrhythmic assemblages. The work also presents itself as conceptual art, enacting ideas of the artwork and artist, and prompting reflections on listening and its varied character. It is as if *MFA* were three or four artworks under the cover of one that, from a traditional point of view, seems barely to inhabit the registers that make music musical—namely, rhythm, melody, and harmony.

Those who favor Eno's gambits, including *MFA*, often credit him with popularizing avant-garde music practices. Bill Martin, for example, has termed him the John Cage of rock, which is apt.[4] Eno's fame is tied as much to what he says as to what he has done musically, and his works enact several concepts. More generally, *MFA* draws upon avant-garde figures and traditions. It is in clear dialogue with composers like Erik Satie, Steve Reich, and La Monte Young and with systems music more broadly. Its attempt to locate art in life also connects it to FLUXUS pieces and performances And, it inhabits a compositional space opened, in part, by the broad sweep of musical history that I have called the sonic turn.

We do *MFA* a disservice, however, if we underestimate how it does more than popularize avant-garde currents. When deployed ambiently, Eno's generative compositions approach everyday life more effectively than works that overly rely on musical performances and performance spaces. His work also manages to celebrate the activity of sounds without paradoxically trying to elude the activities of those who help make them. And at the conceptual level, *MFA* enacts a concept of art that remains immersed within the larger currents that make art possible, which allows one to find nature as well as culture unfolding wherever *MFA* resounds.

By focusing on *MFA* within avant-garde contexts, I may have undersold its pop and rock dimensions, though we did explore how this non-musician developed his skills, whether as a performer (with Roxy Music), producer (with Bowie), or even as a listener (to dub reggae, for instance). But one should not overlook how pop (or rock) and the avant-garde overlap at points. Amateurism is welcome in pop and rock, particularly after punk. But recall its importance to the Scratch Orchestra, and Eno fell in with that lot before he joined Roxy Music. Similarly, while the "activity of sounds" is Cage's calling card, sounding cool or new or unusual is often enough for inclusion in a rock or pop song. "Close enough for rock 'n' roll" could also mean: it just sounds good. In his ambient ventures, I thus find Eno less a crossover figure than someone who works at a crossroads—popular music and the avant-garde, music and painting. And at those intersections, variety results from unplanned interactions. Quite smartly, then, *MFA*'s compositional logic is akin to the logic that organizes Eno's place in the musical landscape of the last fifty years or so: ecological, surprising alignments and juxtapositions, too interesting to ignore. And that is just one more reason why *MFA* is something of a singular achievement, and why it has endured for forty years as something worth revisiting from multiple angles.

ADDITIONAL SOURCES FOR READING AND LISTENING

Ambient 1: Music for Airports can be found on various commercial music servers and on compact disc (Virgin Records, 2004). Bang on a Can's rendition, also available on various commercial servers, offers engaging continuities and contrasts (Point Music, 1998) And for a freer interpretation, listen to Psychic Temple's *Plays Music for Airports* (Joyful Noise Recordings, 2016) *Ambient 4: On Land* provides a sense of Eno's more ecological approach to soundscapes and ambient music (Virgin Records, 2004).

At this point, ambient music is a broad, diverse, and evolving genre. Any of the Pop Ambient samplers (2006–17) curated by Wolfgang Voigt will expose you to a segment of how some inhabit the genre's lighter side (Kompakt Schallplatten). Tomas Köner's "dark ambient" work offers more desolate soundscapes, particularly *Permafrost* (Barooni, 1993). And Aphex Twin's *Selected Ambient Works 85–92* is a reference point for when and how the genre expanded after Eno's initial series (Pias America Classics, 1992). William Basinski's *The Disintegration Loops (Remastered)* offers a site where an emerging ambient-classical tradition can be heard (Temporary Residence, 2012) Finally, *OHM+: the early gurus of electronic music* offers the single best tour of the sonic turn, as well as a booklet (foreword by Eno) and DVD (Elipsis Arts, 2005). A complementary collection can be had in the two-volume *Forbidden Planets* (Chrome Sreams, 2009–11)

There is a world of material surrounding Brian Eno and his music. Two websites are particularly valuable:

- More Dark than Shark: http://www.moredarkthanshark.org
- EnoWeb: http://music.hyperreal.org/artists/brian_eno/index.html

Each hosts transcripts of numerous interviews and articles. Eno also appended several short essays and thought pieces to a diary he kept in 1995 and published as *A Year with Swollen Appendices.* (London: Faber & Faber, 1996) For those seeking a biographical tour of Eno's career, including his ambient ventures, David Sheppard's *On Some Faraway Beach: The Life and Times of Brian Eno* is excellent (London: Orion, 2008). Eric Tamm offers more technical musical assessments in the updated edition of *Brian Eno: His Music and the Vertical Color of Sound* (Boston: Da Capo Press, 1995). For a look at the broader context of the sonic turn, two other studies are particularly valuable. Michael Nyman explores the British scene in *Experimental Music: Cage and Beyond*, 2nd ed. (Cambridge: Cambridge University Press, 1999), For a broad, accessible, and stimulating survey of avant-garde currents in Europe and the United States, see Richard Taruskin's *Music in the Later Twentieth Century,* the final volume in *The Oxford History of Western Music* (Oxford: Oxford University Press, 2010).

NOTES

INTRODUCTION

1 Brian Eno, *Ambient 1 (Music for Airports)* (E.G. Music, 1978).
2 Liner notes to Eno, *Music for Airports.*
3 Milhaud offers the distinction in a memoir. "In any case, the future was to prove Satie right. . . . In all public places, large stores and restaurants the customers are drenched in an unending flood of music. . . . Is this not '*musique d'ameublement*,' heard but not listened to?" Milhaud, *Notes Without Music: An Autobiography*, trans. Donald Evans, ed. Rollo H. Myers (New York: Alfred A. Knopf, 1953), 123.
4 Charley Walters, "Brian Eno—Another Green World," *Rolling Stone*, May 6, 1976.
5 Michael Bloom, "*Ambient 1: Music for Airports*: A Review," *Rolling Stone*, July 26, 1979.
6 Brian Eno, *A Year with Swollen Appendices: Brian Eno's Diary* (London: Faber & Faber, 1996), 296.
7 In Lester Bangs, "Lester Bangs Interviews Brian Eno," *Musician, Player, and Listener*, November 1, 1979, 39.
8 Hewett, "How Brian Eno Created a Quiet Revolution in Music," *Telegraph*, May 20, 2016.
9 The Black Dog, *Music for Real Airports* (Soma Recordings, 2010). The band is quoted in a review published by Resident Advisor, online at https://www.residentadvisor.net/reviews/7404, accessed April 12, 2017.
10 In the liner notes for Psychic Temple, *Psychic Temple Plays Music for Airports* (Joyful Noise Recordings, 2016).
11 In "A Big Theory of Culture: A Talk with Brian Eno," online at https://www.edge.org/conversation/brian_eno-a-big-theory-of-culture, accessed May 12, 2017.

CHAPTER 1

1 Eno recounts this in his essay "The Studio as a Compositional Tool: Part Two" *Downbeat*, August 1983, 52.
2 Eno recounts this in "Generative Music," *In Motion Magazine*, July 7, 1996, online at http://www.inmotionmagazine.com/eno1.html, accessed May 12, 2017.
3 For a more technical discussion of how "1/1" thwarts "whatever desire listeners may have to hear the [piano] line in "1/1" as an expressive melody," see Cecilia Sun, "Resisting the Airport: Bang on a Can Performs Brain Eno," *Musicology Australia* 29 (2007), 153.
4 The painterly nature of many of Eno's compositions has been observed in several locations, including Eric Tamm, *Brain Eno: His Music and the Vertical Color of Sound* (Boston: Da Capo. 1995); Mark Prendergast, *The Ambient Century: From Mahler to Trance; The Evolution of Sound in the Electronic Age* (New York: Bloomsbury, 2000); and Sun, "Resisting the Airport."
5 Quoted on his label's website, http://www.coldbluemusic.com/pages/CB0038.html, and in a review by Jim Fox, online at http://www.textura.org/archives/f/fox_whittington.htm, accessed April 19, 2017.
6 Tamm, *Brian Eno*, 135.

CHAPTER 2

1 Thomas Jerome Seabrook, *Bowie in Berlin: A New Career in a New Town* (London: Jawbone, 2008), 129.
2 Christoph Cox and Daniel Warner, eds., *Audio Culture: Readings in Modern Music* ([New York]: Bloomsbury, 2013), xiii.
3 David Toop, *Oceans of Sound: Aether Talk, Ambient Sound, and Imaginary Worlds* (London: Profile, 1995), 19.
4 Ferruccio Busoni, *A New Esthetic of Music*, trans. T. H. Baker (New York: G. Shirmer, 1911), 24.
5 Arnold Schoenberg, *The Musical Idea and the Logic, Technique, and Art of Its Presentation*, ed. and trans. Patricia Carpenter and Severine Neff (Bloomington: Indiana University Press, 2006), 207–8.
6 The term soundscape comes to us from R. Murray Schafer's studies of the sonic dimensions of cultural life. See R. Murray Schafer, *The Tuning of the World* (New York: Alfred A. Knopf, 1977).
7 In Lawrence Rainey, Christine Poggi, and Laura Wittman, eds., *Futurism: An Anthology*, (New Haven, CT: Yale University Press, 2009), 134.
8 In Rainey, Poggi, and Wittman, *Futurism*, 135.
9 Stefania Serafin has reconstructed the *gracidatore*, "the croaker," and has written extensively on the workings of Intonarumori. See Serafin and Amalia de Götzen,

"An Enactive Approach to the Preservation of Musical Instruments Reconstructing Russolo's Intonarumori," *Journal of New Musical Research* 38 (2009): 231–39.

10 Pierre Schaeffer, *In Search of a Concrete Music* trans. Christine North and John Dack (Berekeley: University of California Press. 2012), 14, 60, 13. Because I have quoted from various points in Schaeffer's First Journal of Concrete Music, 1948–49, I am relying on views that he would grow to modify and contest. But my concern lies less with Schaeffer's evolving view than a few concepts and questions embedded therein. For a philosophically informed account of Schaeffer's conception of the sound object, see Brian Kane, *Sound Unseen: Acousmatic Sound in Theory and Practice* (Oxford: Oxford University Press, 2014).

11 In Rainey, Poggi, and Wittman, *Futurism*, 82.

12 My claim falls in line with Jonathan Sterne's, that sound reproduction technologies worked with and transformed existing practices rather than creating them whole cloth. See Sterne, *The Audible Past: The Cultural Origins of Sound Reproduction* (Durham, NC: Duke University Press, 2003). Another source for a history of that interaction is Evan Eisenberg, *The Recording Angel: Explorations in Phonography* (New York: McGraw Hill, 1987).

13 Edgard Varèse and Chou Wen-chung, "The Liberation of Sound," *Perspectives of New Music* 5 (1966): 18.

14 Edgard Varèse and Alcopley, "Edgard Varèse on Music and Art: A Conversation between Varèse and Alcopley," *Leonardo* 1 (April 1968): 192.

15 Varèse and Chou, "Liberation of Sound," 11. Discussing a later ambient work, *Thursday Afternoon*, Eno has spoken of an "unfolding display of unique sonic clusters." Quoted in Anthony Denselow, "Over and Over," *Observer*, February 23, 1986.

16 Richard Taruskin, *The Oxford History of Western Music*, vol. 5, *The Late Twentieth Century* (Oxford: Oxford University Press, 2005), 210.

17 Jim Aikin, "Eno," *Keyboard*, July 1981, 52.

18 The address was "The Future of Music: Credo," which Cage delivered in Seattle in 1937. It became the first essay in his celebrated book *Silence: Lectures and Writings* (Middletown, CT: Wesleyan University Press, 1961).

19 Michael Nyman, *Experimental Music: Cage and Beyond*, 2nd ed. (Cambridge: Cambridge University Press, 1999), 4.

20 In David Sheppard, *On Some Faraway Beach: The Life and Times of Brian Eno* (London: Orion, 2008), 276.

21 Cage, *Silence*, 59.

22 Alvin Lucier and Douglas Simon, *Chambers* (Middletown, CT: Weslyan University Press,1980), 37.

23 La Monte Young, "Lecture 1960," *Tulane Drama Review* 10, no. 2 (Winter 1965): 80–81.
24 In Willaim Duckworth, *Talking Music* (New York: Schirmer, 1995), 228.
25 In Duckworth, *Talking Music*, 241.
26 Jeremy Grimshaw, *Draw a Straight Line and Follow It: The Music and Mysticism of La Monte Young* (Oxford: Oxford University Press. 2011), 18.
27 Ronald M. Radano, "Jazzin' the Classics: The AACM's Challenge to Mainstream Aesthetics," *Black Music Research Journal* 12, no. 1 (Spring 1992): 79–95.
28 These trends and others are discussed by Joanna Demers in *Listening through the Noise: The Aesthetics of Experimental Electronic Music* (Oxford: Oxford University Press, 2010).

CHAPTER 3

1 Nick Kent, "Last Tango in Amsterdam," *New Musical Express*, June 9, 1973, 5.
2 In Rob Tannenbaum, "A Meeting of Sound Minds: John Cage + Brian Eno," *Musician*, September 1, 1985, 69.
3 In Jim Aikin, "Eno," *Keyboard*, July 1981, 52–53.
4 In Bill Milkowski, "Eno: Excursions in the Electronic Environment," *Down Beat*, June 1983.
5 In Aikin, "Eno," 52.
6 In Lester Bangs, "ENO," *Musician, Player, and Listener.* 1979. 42.
7 In Ian Macdonald, "Under the Influence: Brian Eno Speaks about his Musical Progenitors," *New Musical Express*, March 10, 1973 (emphasis added).
8 In Aikin, "Eno," 55.
9 In Aikin, "Eno," 52.
10 One can read an overlapping account, with a look at parallels in computer development, in Steve Dietz, "Learning from Eno," in Christopher Scoates, *Brian Eno: Visual Music* (San Francisco: Chronicle, 2013), 288–305.
11 David Sheppard, *On Some Faraway Beach: The Life and Times of Brian Eno* (London: Orion, 2008), 13.
12 Sheppard, *On Some Faraway Beach*, 29.
13 For a recounting of this time, see Scoates, *Brian Eno*, 23–32. Eno's remark about not wanting a job appears in his conversation with Lester Bangs, in Bangs, "Brian Eno: A Sandbox in Alphaville," available online at http://www.moredarkthanshark.org/eno_int_perso-sepoct03.html, accessed June 6, 2017. Eno's remark is repeated in Sasha Frere-Jones, "Ambient Genius," *New Yorker*, July 7, 2014.

14 In Lucy O'Brien, "How We Met: Brian Eno and Tom Philips," *Independent*, September 13, 1998.

15 Ian MacDonald, "Thinking About Music with Brian Eno: Part One," *New Musical Express*, November 26, 1977.

16 Roy Ascott, "Behaviorist Art and the Cybernetic Vision," *Cybernetica: Journal of the International Association of Cybernetics* 9, no. 4 (1966): 97.

17 A discussion of Eno and cybernetics can also be found in Geeta Dayal, *Another Green World* (New York: Bloomsbury, 2009).

18 In Scoates, *Brian Eno*, 26.

19 In Frank Rose, "Scaramouche of the Synthesizer," *Creem*, July 1975, 30.

20 Eno recounted this idea in a letter to the cybernetic theorist and consultant Stafford Beer (1926–2002). The letter is reproduced in Scoates, *Brian Eno*, 100.

21 Cybernetics remained part of this conversation as well. In 1968, the London Institute of Art hosted *Cybernetic Serendipity*, whose musical director was Peter Schmidt, Eno's later friend and collaborator. The exhibition led to an album of computer music, which included work by Cage. See Dietz, "Learning from Eno," 289.

22 In William Duckworth, *Talking Music* (New York: Schirmer, 1995), 239.

23 In Bangs, "Brian Eno."

24 In Bangs, "Brian Eno."

25 In MacDonald, "Under the Influence."

26 That Eno entered rock 'n' roll already a non-musician is evidenced by his modestly and privately printed—but now lost—pamphlet, "Music for Non-Musicians," which appeared in 1970. See Sheppard, *On Some Faraway Beach*, 67.

27 Michael Nyman, *Experimental Music: Cage and Beyond*, 2nd ed. (Cambridge: Cambridge University Press, 1999), 115.

28 In Sheppard, *On Some Faraway Beach*, 63.

29 The essay is reprinted in Brian Eno, *A Year with Swollen Appendices: Brian Eno's Diary* (London: Faber & Faber, 1996), 333–44.

30 Brian Eno, "Generative Music," *In Motion Magazine*, July 7, 1996, http://www.inmotionmagazine.com/eno1.html, accessed May 12, 2017.

31 Eno, "Generative Music."

32 Steve Reich, *Writings on Music: 1965–2000*, ed. Paul Hillier (Oxford: Oxford University Press, 2002) 14, 19.

33 Eno, "Generative Music."

34 John Cage, *Silence: Lectures and Writings* (Middletown, CT: Wesleyan University Press, 1961), 10.

35 Rob Chapman, "Roxy Music: They Came from Planet Bacofoil," *Mojo*, December 1995, available online at http://www.rob-chapman.com/pages/journalism.html, accessed April 29, 2017.

36 Sheppard, *On Some Faraway Beach*, 72.

37 Sheppard, *On Some Faraway Beach*, 75.

38 Gordon Reid, "All About EMS: Parts 1 & 2," *Sound on Sound*, November/December 2000.

39 In Chapman, "Roxy Music." One can hear the introduction of ambience and atmosphere even more so on the next Roxy album, *For Your Pleasure*, particularly on the track "The Bogus Man," where Ferry's vocals are echoed and stretched and nearly everything sounds treated.

40 David Pattie suggests that the split resulted from very different aesthetic sensibilities. Whereas Ferry wished to restage existing forms, Eno wanted to present music that incorporated chance. Pattie, "The Bogus Men: Eno, Ferry, and Roxy Music," in *Brian Eno: Oblique Music*, ed. Sean Albiez and David Pattie (London: Bloomsbury Academic. 2016), 11–27.

41 Sheppard, *On Some Faraway Beach*, 103, 141.

42 According to Fripp, Eno coined the title "Swastika Girls" after seeing the phrase on a magazine page lying upon the pavement. The title seems purposefully unrelated to the track, so as to remove any thought of programmatic content. See Scott Cohen, "Fripp and Eno: No Pussyfooting Around," *Hit Parade*, June 1974.

43 In Andy Gill, "The Oblique Strategist," *Mojo*, June 1995.

44 Eno's remark can be found in "Painting with Sound" (10′40″–10′48″), the second episode of *Soundbreaking: Stories from the Edge of Recorded Music*, prod. Jeff Dupre, ed. Nancy Novak and Jay Keuper (2016). Maren's appeared in Roger Maren, "Music by Montage and Mixing," *The Reporter*, October 6, 1955, 38.

45 In Brian Eno, "The Studio as a Compositional Tool: Part Two," *Downbeat*, August 1983, 52.

46 In Sheppard, *On Some Faraway Beach*, 260.

47 Alongside Sheppard's *On Some Faraway Beach* and Eric Tamm's *Brian Eno: His Music and the Vertical Color of Sound* (Boston: Da Capo. 1995), there is Thomas Seabrook's *Bowie in Berlin: A New Career in a New Town* (London: Jawbone, 2008) and Dayal's *Another Green World*. For an intriguing survey of Eno's studio efforts between 1973 and 1977, also see David Pattie, "Taking the Studio by Strategy," in Albiez and Pattie, *Brian Eno*, 49–68.

48 In Brian Eno, "The Studio as a Compositional Tool: Part One," *Downbeat*, July, 1983, 57.

49 In Eno, "The Studio as a Compositional Tool: Part Two," 51.

50 Cecilia Sun, "Brian Eno, Non-Musicianship and Experimental Tradition," in Albiez and Pattie, *Brian Eno*, 32.

51 In Kenneth Ansell, "Eno," part 2, *Impetus* 4 (ca. 1976), 166.

52 In Aikin, "Eno," 56. For an illuminating discussion of how Eno's time in the Portsmouth Sinfonia affected his manner of being a non-musician, see Sun, "Brian Eno," 34–38.

53 Adrian Jack, "I Want to Be a Magnet for Tapes," *Time Out*, March 15–18, 1975, and Tom Johnson, "Gavin Bryar's Work Is Good Four Ways," *Village Voice*, August 2, 1976. Eno is quoted in Ansell, "Eno," part 2.

54 Eno noted this similarity in conversation with Ian MacDonald in an interview from 1977. See MacDonald, "Thinking About Music with Brian Eno: Part One," *New Musical Express*, November 26, 1977.

55 Notably, the principle of inclusion for the Obscure series was "not whether I think it's important or not; it's whether I like it or not." See Ansell, "Eno," 100.

56 In Jack, "I Want to Be a Magnet."

CHAPTER 4

1 In Ian MacDonald, "Thinking About Music with Brian Eno: Part One," *New Musical Express*, November 26, 1977.

2 In David Sheppard, *On Some Faraway Beach: The Life and Times of Brian Eno* (London: Orion, 2008), 189.

3 In "Memoirs of an Amnesic," Satie declares: "Anyone will tell you that I am not a musician. They are right." *A Mammal's Notebook: The Writings of Erik Satie*, ed. Ornella Volta, trans. Antony Melville (London: Atlas, 2014), 108.

4 Darius Milhaud, *Notes Without Music: An Autobiography*, ed. Rollo H. Myers, trans. Donald Evans (New York: Alfred A. Knopf, 1953), 123.

5 In Pierre-Daniel Templier, *Erik Satie* (Cambridge, MA: MIT Press, 1969), 45.

6 I am drawing in this paragraph from Templier, *Erik Satie*, and Satie, *Mammal's Notebook*.

7 Hubert Unverricht and Cliff Eisen, "Divertimento," in *Grove Music Online* (Oxford University Press), accessed February 11, 2017.

8 Anthony Korner, "Aurora Musicalis," *ARTFORUM* (Summer 1986), 77.

9 Liner notes to Brian Eno, *Ambient 1: Music for Airports*.

10 Henry Jenkins, "On Brian Eno and Barry Lyndon: An Interview with Geeta Dayal (Part One)," *Confessions of an Aca-Fan*, March 15, 2010, anline at http://henryjenkins.org/2010/03/on_brian_eno_and_barry_lyndon.html, accessed March 29, 2017.

11 John Cage, *Silence: Lectures and Writings* (Middletown, CT: Wesleyan University Press, 1961), 80.

12 Cage, *Silence*, 82.

13 In Satie, *Mammal's Notebook*, 216.

14 My continuum builds upon David Toop's claim, that ambient music has two principal forms: music made from environment sounds and music that aims to fit into an environment. See Toop, *Oceans of Sound: Aether Talk, Ambient Sound, and Imaginary Worlds* (London: Profile, 1995), 197–98.

15 Toop, *Oceans of Sound*, 198.

16 Brian Eno, *A Year with Swollen Appendices: Brian Eno's Diary* (London: Faber & Faber, 1996), 294.

17 Liner notes to Brian Eno, *Ambient 4 (On Land)* (E. G. Records, 1982).

18 Pauline Oliveros, *Deep Listening: A Composer's Sound Practice* (New York: iUniverse, 2005), xxiv.

19 In Satie, *Mammal's Notebook*, 216.

20 To capture the character of these barren-scapes, Kevin Martin has conceptualized a subgenre of ambient, "isolationism," which Simon Reynolds regards as "ice-olationist, offering cold comfort." Simon Reynolds, "Chill: The New Ambient," *Artforum*, January 1995.

21 Liner notes to Max Richter, *From Sleep* (Deutsche Grammophon, 2015).

22 Toop, *Oceans of Sound*, 54.

23 A transcript of a radio conversation from the show *Paul Merton's Hour of Silence*, broadcast January 1, 1995, available online at http://music.hyperreal.org/artists/brian_eno/interviews/ambe2.html, accessed June 13, 2017.

24 For a readable history of the FLUXUS movement, see Owen. F. Smith, *Fluxus: The History of an Attitude* (San Diego: San Diego State University Press, 1998).

25 Brecht's scores, alongside many others by FLUXUS artists, can be found in Ken Friedman, Owen Smith, and Lauren Sawchyn, eds., *Fluxus Performance Workbook* (Performance Research E-publications, 2002), 21.

26 The history of Muzak and analogous ventures is recounted in Joseph Lanza, *Elevator Music: A Surreal History of Muzak, Easy-Listening, and Other Moodsong* (New York: St. Martin's, 1994).

27 Lanza, *Elevator Music*, 41.

28 Lanza, *Elevator Music*, 86.

29 Eno's observations can be found in his foreword to Mark Prendergast, *The Ambient Century from Mahler to Trance: The Evolution of Sound in the Electronic Age* (New York: Bloomsbury, 2000), xii.

30 Lanza, *Elevator Music*, 69.

31 Nick Kent, "A Flight of Fantasy," *New Musical Express*, February 3, 1972, 5.

32 In Steve Peacock, "Roxy: What Next—A Marching Band?" *Sounds*, January 27, 1973.

33 Prendergast, *Ambient Century*, xi.

34 Eno, *A Year*, 295.

35 Sheppard, *On Some Faraway Beach*, 279.

36 Liner notes to Eno, *Music for Airports* (emphasis added).

37 In Anthony Korner, "Aurora Musicalis," *Artforum*, Summer 1986, 77.

38 Morse Peckham, *Man's Rage for Chaos: Biology, Behavior, and the Arts* (Philadelphia: Chilton, 1965), xi.

39 Peckham, *Man's Rage for Chaos*, xi.

40 Each of the chapters in Dayal's *Another Green World* (New York: Bloomsbury, 2009) is named after an oblique strategy.

41 David Sterrit, "The 'Furniture Music' of Rock Star Brian Eno," *Christian Science Monitor*, May 3, 1984.

42 Toop, *Oceans of Sound*, iv. Describing *MFA* as a whole, David Sheppard also employs the term. "Together the four tracks comprised forty-eight minutes of blissfully weightless reverie." Sheppard, *On Some Faraway Beach*, 278.

43 In Allan Jones, "Eno—Class of 1975," *Melody Maker*, November 29, 1975, 14.

44 Toop, *Oceans of Sound*, 178.

45 Michael Fried, *Art and Objecthood: Essays and Reviews* (Chicago: University of Chicago Press, 1998).

46 Anahid Kassabian, *Ubiquitous Listening: Affect, Attention, and Distributed Subjectivity* (Berkeley: University of California Press, 2013), 27.

47 For my account of sense of self, see Paul Lysaker and John Lysaker, *Schizophrenia and the Fate of the Self* (Oxford: Oxford University Press, 2008), chap. 3, and John Lysaker, *After Emerson* (Bloomington: Indiana University Press, 2017), chap. 4.

48 Gilles Deleuze and Félix Guattari, *A Thousand Plateaus: Capitalism and Schizophrenia*, trans. Brian Massumi (Minneapolis: University of Minnesota Press, 1987). For a reading of *MFA* from the standpoint of Deleuze and Guattari's work, see my "Turning Listening Inside Out: Brian Eno's *Ambient1: Music for Airports*," *Journal of Speculative Philosophy* 31, no. 1 (2017): 155–176.

CHAPTER 5

1 Quoted in Stephen Anthony Barr, "Pleasure is the law": *Pelléas et Mélisande* as Debussy's Decisive Shift Away from Wagnerism" (PhD diss., West Virginia Universisty, 2007), 68–69.

2 Lawrence Weiner, *Statements* (New York: Seth Siegellaub & the Louis Kellner Foundation, 1968), not paginated.

3 Lawrence Weiner's statement of intent states: "1. The artist may construct the piece 2. The piece may be fabricated 3. The piece need not be built." Seth Sigellaub, ed., *January 5–31, 1969: Exhibition Catalogue* (New York: Seth Siegellaub, 1969), not paginated.

4 The first report I know is John Foxx's brief reflection piece from 2011: "Music for Airports: An Appreciation by John Foxx," *The List*, October 19, 2011.

5 Steve Reich, *Writings on Music: 1965–2000*, ed. Paul Hiller (New York: Oxford University Press, 2002), 34.
6 Reich, *Writings on Music*, 32.
7 Reich, *Writings on Music*, 35. Sun discusses the relation of *Discreet Music* to Reich's approach to the gradual process in "Brian Eno, Non-Musicianship and Experimental Tradition," in *Brian Eno: Oblique Music*, ed. Sean Albiez and David Pattie (London: Bloomsbury Academic, 2016), 45.
8 Brian Eno, "Generative Music," *Motion Magazine*, July 7, 1996.
9 Rob Tannenbaum, "A Meeting of Sound Minds: John Cage + Brian Eno," *Musician*, September 1, 1985. 68.
10 Tannenbaum, "Meeting of Sound Minds."
11 Eno, "Generative Music."
12 Liner notes to John White and Gavin Bryars, *Machine Music* (Obscure Records, 1978).
13 Brian Dennis, "The Music of John White," *Musical Times* 112 (1971): 437.
14 Ian MacDonald, "Thinking about Music with Brian Eno. Part Two: How to Make a Modern Record," *New Musical Express*, December 3, 1977.
15 Brian Eno, "Composers as Gardeners," *Edge*, October 11, 2011, online at https://www.edge.org/conversation/brian_eno-composers-as-gardeners, accessed March 5, 2017. In presenting his most recent ambient album, *Reflection* (2017), Eno has also relied upon a gardening metaphor.
16 Per Michael Nyman, Earle Brown affirmed a similarly interactive conception of the work, regarding "form as a function of people acting directly in response to a described environment," which led him believe it "reasonable to consider the potential of the human mind as a collaborative creative parameter." Nyman. *Experimental Music: Cage and Beyond*, 2nd ed. (Cambridge: Cambridge University Press, 1999), 57.
17 In Anthony Korner, "Aurora Musicalis," *Artforum*, Summer 1986, 78. (I am also drawing upon this article in recounting the logic of *Living Room*.) Referring to a later work for DVD, *77 Million Paintings* (2006), Eno also employs the analogy of organic life. "Evolution and organic growth dictate the life of this piece and we can only accept its presence and watch it unfold." Quoted in Christopher Scoates, *Brian Eno: Visual Music* (San Francisco: Chronicle, 2013, 341.
18 Brian Dillon, "Gone to Earth," in Scoates, *Brian Eno*, 197.
19 Liner notes to the DVD *Brian Eno: 14 Paintings*. (Hannibal Records, 2005). The DVD contains "Mistaken Memories of Medieval New York" and "Thursday Afternoon."
20 Liner notes to *Brian Eno: 14 Paintings*. Eno even draws a parallel between his manipulations of the camera's light sensitivity to the use of an "expander" in the studio, which lowers the volume of the quietest tones and increases the volume of louder ones, amplifying the tracks' dynamic range.

21 One might also pursue more general philosophical questions at this point, taking "listening" as a basic way in which we inhabit the world. Given that our focus is *MFA*, such a discussion would prove distracting if interesting. For those interested in such a discussion, consult Veit Erlman, *Reason and Resonance: A History of Modern Aurality* (New York: Zone, 2014); Jean-Luc Nancy, *Listening*, trans. Charlotte Mandell (New York: Fordham University Press, 2007); and Peter Szendy, *Listen: A History of Our Ears.* trans. Charlotte Mandell (New York: Fordham University Press, 2008).

22 Joseph Lanza, *Elevator Music: A Surreal History of Muzak, Easy-Listening, and Other Moodsong* (New York: St. Martin's, 1994), 165. For a fascinating study of music's possible impact on well-being, see Tia DeNora, *Music Asylums: Wellbeing Through Music in Everyday Life* (Farnham, UK: Ashgate, 2015).

23 Joanna Demers, *Listening Through the Noise: The Aesthetics of Experimental Electronic Music* (Oxford: Oxford University Press, 2010), 151–52.

24 Demers, *Listening Through the Noise*, 16.

25 Defining "adequate listening," Ola Stockfelt says, "It means that one masters and develops the ability to listen for what is relevant to the genre in the music, for what is adequate to understanding . . . the specific genre's comprehensible context." Stockfelt, "Adequate Modes of Listening," in *Keeping Score: Music, Disciplinarity, Culture*, ed. David Schwarrtz, Anahid Kassabian, and Lawrence Siegel (Charlottesville: University of Virginia Press, 1997), 137.

26 Adorno introduces and develops this concept in "On the Fetish Character in Music and the Regression of Listening," in *The Essential Frankfurt School Reader*, ed. Andrew Arator and Eike Gebhardt (New York: Continuum, 1982), 270–99.

27 Eno addressed just this issue with his release of *77 Million Paintings* (2006), which he described as a "slow changing light painting" in an interview disc that accompanies the work. Eno, *77 Million Paintings by Brian Eno* (Hannibal Records, 2006). Lamenting that many of his installations force people to seek out museum and gallery spaces, he released *77 Million Paintings* as a CD-ROM for video screens in the hope that it might bring beauty and interest to television screens that lie mostly dormant in people's homes. Intriguingly, Roger Maren in 1955 already saw the same potential in the phonograph. See Maren, "Music by Montage and Mixing," *Reporter*, October 6, 1955, 42.

28 Pauline Oliveros, *Deep Listening: A Composer's Sound Practice* (New York: iUniverse, 2005), 13.

29 David Grubbs. *Records Ruin the Landscape: John Cage, the Sixties, and Sound Recording* (Durham, NC: Duke University Press, 2014), 96).

30 This founding purpose is articulated repeatedly in the documentary *In the Ocean*, directed by Frank Scheffer (Allegiri Film, 2000).

31 A live recording appeared ten years later, followed by a DVD in 2009 that paired the music with four airport-themed video-art pieces by Frank Scheffer, which accompanied the Bang on a Can All-Stars performing *MFA* at the Holland Festival in 1999 in the arrival area of an airport. See Scheffer, *Brian Eno: Music for Airports & In the Ocean* (Euro Arts, 2009).

32 Michael Gordon can be heard saying this off-camera in Scheffer's documentary, *In the Ocean*, 37′10″–37′25″.

33 In Scheffer's documentary *In the Ocean*, 38′20″–38′36″.

34 In correspondence, Ziporyn shared that the opening convergence of clarinet and bass was "written with the idea that it was an opportunity for Robert Black and me to make a sound together" (pers. comm., February 2, 2017).

35 Cecilia Sun argues that one cannot find this kind of development in the original, and she further explains how Ziporyn introduces his, from extending the overall length of the piece to creating cadences by extending the duration of certain phrases. See Sun, "Resisting the Airport: Bang on a Can Performs Brain Eno," *Musicology Australia* 29 (2007): 154.

36 Sun observes another dimension of this transformation. In particular, she argues that Bang on a Can's interpretation also draws Eno's album into a musical history that valorizes and even insists upon virtuosity and structural complexity as integral to music. See Sun, "Resisting the Airport."

37 In "Generative Music," Eno mentions the existence of a thirty-minute version of "1/2." Eno, "Generative Music," *In Motion Magazine*, July 7, 1996, http://www.inmotionmagazine.com/eno1.html, accessed May 12, 2017.

CROSSROADS

1 In Pat Thomas, "3+1: An Interview with Jon Hassell," in the liner notes for the 2014 re-release of *Possible Musics* (Glitterbeat Records, 2014).

2 In Ed Ward, Geoffrey Stokes, and Ken Tucker, *Rock of Ages: The Rolling Stone History of Rock & Roll* (New York: Rolling Stone Press, 1986), 490. Gavin Bryars has also joined the "can't play" chorus. See David Sheppard, *On Some Faraway Beach: The Life and Times of Brian Eno* (London: Orion, 2008), 5.

3 In Lester Bangs, "Lester Bangs Interviews Brian Eno," *Musician, Player, and Listener*, November 1, 1979, 39.

4 Bill Martin, *Avant Rock: Experimental Music from the Beatles to Björk* (Chicago: Open Court, 2002), 104.

INDEX

www.ingramcontent.com/pod-product-compliance
Ingram Content Group UK Ltd.
Pitfield, Milton Keynes, MK11 3LW, UK
UKHW041845200726
13854UKWH00005BA/2180